Praise for *The GCSE Mindset*

The GCSE Mindset is an excellent book packed with a wide range of exercises. The authors have done a fantastic job of coherently pulling together a vast array of helpful tools and in doing so have compiled a comprehensive guide for teachers in their quest to support pupils striving for academic success.

Dr Steve Bull, Performance Psychologist and Executive Coach, GamePlanCoach

The GCSE Mindset builds ably on the best of its precursor, *The A Level Mindset*, which proved so popular with heads of sixth form. The depth and detail is both a strength and a challenge as it will take dedicated staff at Key Stage 4 time to digest it, but if they are keen to improve outcomes and build skills then they, and their students, will be rewarded with a richly supportive tutorial scheme that will have an impact on exam results.

Year 10 and 11 assemblies, as well as tutorial time, have been waiting for *The GCSE Mindset*. This material is no fad and is here to stay for some time, as the thought and breadth of the book's practical strategies are the result of the wealth of research and talent of two experienced practitioners, Steve Oakes and Martin Griffin. Get yourself a copy – you won't be disappointed!

Michael Senior, CEO, Netsixthform.co.uk

In *The GCSE Mindset* Steve Oakes and Martin Griffin pose the question, 'How can the theory be put into practice?' and, in the same accessible way as in *The A Level Mindset*, they show you exactly how to do just that.

Kevin Green, Principal, Manchester Health Academy

I have worked with over twenty sixth forms to introduce some of the ideas behind *The A Level Mindset* and we are now beginning to see its activities and approaches pay real dividends, so it was with great anticipation that I read *The GCSE Mindset* and considered how the previous approaches could be applied to students at Key Stage 4. What Steve Oakes and Martin Griffin do in this book is make sense of the research into areas such as meta-cognition and growth mindset and come up with a practical and no-nonsense approach to supporting students' learning through the GCSE years.

As the authors point out, in too many schools our students have become 'passive learners' in such a way that short-changes them and their progress. As a consequence, schools often fail to develop in students the skills and mindset they will need in their future academic and working lives. The focus of *The GCSE Mindset*, put very simply, is to tackle the question, 'How do we make better learners?' and the authors provide a thorough and thought-provoking attempt at addressing this issue.

Their VESPA system provides a clear umbrella under which schools can reflect on how they support student learning – so that rather than teachers pushing students, the students themselves develop their own approach to pull through their GCSE years. The authors provide a whole host of concise and practical activities that develop effective systems for learning, offer scaffolding for the setting of meaningful short- and long-term goals, and lay out what effective practice and revision really looks like. One of the changes from *The A Level Mindset* is to tackle the GCSE year on a month-by-month basis, tailoring activities to particular challenges and demands during this period. This is easily adapted to schools' own experiences and it aims to support student learning more effectively; so in the run-up to mock examinations, for example, the focus is upon practice and resilience.

The activities themselves are brilliant, fun and engaging: each has a clear purpose, is easily adaptable to individual schools' needs, and will encourage students to reflect upon their own learning as well as equip them with essential skills for GCSE study.

The GCSE Mindset is a really timely book that will help all schools facing the challenges of GCSEs' linear assessment and the huge demands in terms of content to be learnt and the sheer number of hours now spent focusing on examinations. If nothing else, it forces all schools to ask some very serious questions about how they deliver the GCSE programme to their students, and how they nurture the skills required for success and the coping strategies needed within a more stressful assessment culture.

Mark Fuller, Sixth Form Consultant, Girls' Day School Trust

A timely resource given the increasing interest in essential life skills and students' well-being, this well-written book provides a wide range of beneficial activities to help students achieve their full potential and develop lifelong learning capabilities.

Steve Oakes and Martin Griffin have carefully drawn on research evidence and combined this with their extensive practical knowledge to create an informative guide for teachers, parents and GCSE students. With the pressurised and demanding education system we currently have, it is imperative that we support our young people to develop resilience and grit, and to manage and organise their learning effectively. *The GCSE Mindset* offers an excellent starting point for achieving this.

Professor Cathy Lewin, Manchester Metropolitan University

The GCSE Mindset

40 activities for transforming student commitment, motivation and productivity

Steve Oakes and Martin Griffin

Crown House Publishing Limited
www.crownhouse.co.uk

First published by
Crown House Publishing
Crown Buildings,
Bancyfelin,
Carmarthen,
Wales, SA33 5ND, UK
www.crownhouse.co.uk
and
Crown House Publishing Company LLC
PO Box 2223, Williston, VT 05495, USA
www.crownhousepublishing.com

First published 2017. Reprinted 2018, 2019.

Page 5, Figure 0.1 © Jubilee Centre for Character and Virtues (2017). *A Framework for Character Education in Schools* (Birmingham: Jubilee Centre for Character and Virtues). Available at: http://www.jubileecentre.ac.uk/userfiles/jubileecentre/pdf/character-education/Framework%20for%20Character%20Education.pdf. Reproduced with permission. Page 12, Figure 0.4 © Farrington, C. A., Roderick, M., Allensworth, E., Nagaoka, J., Keyes, T. S., Johnson, D. W. and Beechum, N. O. (2012). *Teaching Adolescents to Become Learners: The Role of Non-Cognitive Factors on Shaping School Performance: A Critical Literature Review* (Chicago, IL: University of Chicago Consortium on Chicago School Research), p. 4. Reproduced with permission. Page 100, extract © Schwarzer, R. and Jerusalem, M. (1995). Generalized self-efficacy scale. In J. Weinman, S. Wright and M. Johnston (eds), *Measures in Health Psychology: A User's Portfolio. Causal and Control Beliefs* (Windsor: NFER-Nelson), pp. 35–37. Reproduced with permission. Page 107, extract © Bull, S. (2006). *The Game Plan: Your Guide to Mental Toughness at Work* (Chichester: Capstone Publishing), p. 125. Used with permission. Page 128, Figure © Max Landsberg, 2003. *The Tao of Coaching: Boost your Effectiveness at Work by Inspiring and Developing Those Around You*, 2nd edn (London: Profile Books). Used with permission. Pages 142–143 © Jennifer McGahan. Used with permission.

British Library Cataloguing-in-Publication Data

A catalogue entry for this book is available from the British Library.

Print ISBN: 978-178583184-3
Mobi ISBN: 978-178583287-1
ePub ISBN: 978-178583288-8
ePDF ISBN: 978-178583289-5
LCCN 2017955414

Printed and bound in the UK by Gomer Press, Llandysul, Ceredigion

Authors' Note

Education has always been a battleground of ideas. Follow a couple of hundred educators on social media and within a few days you'll be witnessing – who knows, perhaps even becoming embroiled in – arguments about the purpose and process of education. Effect sizes are in; effect sizes are out. Studies can be replicated and peer reviewed; a few weeks later they can't. Character education was in – now it's 'essential life skills'. Evidence-based teaching is everything, then intuitive common sense and good teacher–pupil relationships are key. Carol Dweck is a hero, or emphatically not. Sometimes it seems that all we can agree on is that learning styles don't exist. (Except – deep breath – maybe they do.) These passionate and principled viewpoints, and the discussion that buzzes around them, are important. We're all trying to become better at what we do and help pupils become better at what they do. But sometimes these arguments result in paralysis. If every theory, approach and study in the world can be debunked by one that proves the opposite, we have stasis; a discussion paralysed by an over-abundance of information. So we carry on as before until something demonstrably better arrives, and that helps no one.

The resources that follow are not a partisan polemic allied to a specific way of thinking – we've borrowed liberally from as many studies as we could. This book doesn't represent a silver bullet either. But it does emerge from a combined forty years of teaching, tutoring, coaching, intervening and cajoling young learners forward in seven different institutions. We've since met, talked with and presented to thousands of people (staff and pupils) working in hundreds of schools and colleges across the UK and noticed this: despite our tendency as teachers to almost mythologise the specific challenges of our particular micro-contexts, wherever we go, young people face the same personal issues and challenges, fight the same battles of will and discipline, and experience very similar victories and setbacks.

Bearing all this in mind, we hope that you find something of use in this book. Ignore the material that doesn't work for you, focus on the stuff that does and make as many alterations, adjustments and wholesale overhauls as you need to – and try to steer clear of those Twitter-storms too!

We might be the people who have hammered away putting these words on the page, but a book is the work of many hands. It's almost ten years since we started working together. What started as a weekly early morning coffee meeting to discuss our ideas has developed into something far bigger than we could ever have envisaged. There are so many people who we've spoken to and who have helped shape our thinking. Thanks to Ben White for the erudite and analytical conversation, for developing ideas about leading and lagging indicators through discussion, and, of course, for the beer. Thanks to Neil Dagnall and Andrew Denovan for contributing Chapter 14: Measuring Mindset Using Psychometric Tests. Thanks to Lucy Parsons for her seemingly limitless enthusiasm for supporting students and for giving us the time and space to talk about our work. Thanks to Jennifer McGahan for the practice activity Test Yourself! We would also like to take this opportunity to thank everyone at Crown House, in particular, David Bowman for his unwavering support of all our ideas, Rosalie Williams for dealing with countless random emails and the whole of the brilliant production team who've worked tirelessly finishing this project to the highest standards!

We have made every attempt to recognise the work of those who have inspired many of the ideas and concepts that we have used in this book. We would, of course, like to make particular reference to the work of Carol Dweck and Angela Duckworth for inspiring us to develop this system, and to thank the many teachers and pupils who have listened, experimented, commented, criticised and helped us tweak (and sometimes just ditch!) the tools we've developed.

@VESPAmindset

VESPAmindset.com

Contents

Authors' Note | i

Introduction | 1

Chapter 1
The VESPA Model:
An Introduction to VESPA | 15

Chapter 2
Using This Book | 31

Chapter 3
September: Start with the Why | 35

1. Vision Activity: The Motivation
   Diamond | 39
2. Vision Activity: Problem Not Job,
   aka The Personal Compass | 41
3. Effort Activity: Mission and Medal | 43
4. Attitude Activity: Growth Mindset | 47

Chapter 4
October: Mapping the Journey | 51

5. Vision Activity: The Roadmap | 56
6. Systems Activity: The Weekly
   Planner | 58
7. Vision Activity: The Rule of Three | 60
8. Systems Activity: Chunking Steps | 62
9. Vision Activity: Grit | 64

Chapter 5
November: Leading and
Lagging Indicators | 67

10. Practice Activity: Building Independent
    Learning | 71
11. Systems Activity: Three Types of
    Attention | 74
12. Attitude Activity: Network Audits | 76
13. Effort Activity: Looking Under the Rocks,
    aka Four Steps Forward | 78

Chapter 6
December: The Three Phases
of Practice | 81

14. Practice Activity: The Practice
    Questionnaire | 86
15. Effort Activity: The Three 'Hows' of
    Independent Work | 88
16. Practice Activity: It's Time to Teach,
    aka CASTT | 90
17. Vision Activity: Setting a Personal
    Best | 93
18. Vision Activity: Success Leaves
    Clues | 95

Contents

Chapter 7
January: Agency and Efficacy | **97**

19. Vision Activity: Five Roads | 102

20. Vision Activity: The Ten-Year Grid | 104

21. Attitude Activity: The Battery | 107

22. Systems Activity: The Bottom Left | 109

23. Attitude Activity: Managing Reactions to Feedback | 111

Chapter 8
February: Effort is Relative | **113**

24. Effort Activity: The Effort Thermometer | 119

25. Effort Activity: Packing My Bags | 121

26. Effort Activity: Twenty-Five Minute Sprints | 123

27. Practice Activity: The Nine-Box Grid | 125

28. Practice Activity: Will vs. Skill | 127

Chapter 9
March: Fight or Flight | **131**

29. Attitude Activity: The Problem Solving Cycle | 136

30. Practice Activity: K-SPA | 138

31. Practice Activity: Spaced Practice | 140

32. Practice Activity: Test Yourself! | 142

33. Vision Activity: What's Stopping You? | 144

Chapter 10
April: Changing Lanes, Finding Flow | **149**

34. Practice Activity: Finding Flow | 155

35. Practice Activity: High Flow Spaces | 159

36. Vision Activity: Now vs. Most | 162

37. Systems Activity: The Action Priority Matrix | 165

38. Attitude Activity: Benefit Finding, aka The Rocky Road | 168

Chapter 11
May: Well-Being and Stress Management | **171**

39. Attitude Activity: The First Aid Kit – Three Exercises to Dissolve Stress | 175

40. Effort Activity: Pre-Making Decisions | 178

Chapter 12
Coaching with VESPA | **181**

Chapter 13
Implementation: Putting VESPA into Action | **193**

Chapter 14
Measuring Mindset Using Psychometric Tests by Neil Dagnall and Andrew Denovan | **211**

Conclusion:
Ten Final Thoughts | **225**

References | 229

Index | 237

Introduction

Numerous instances can be cited of people with high IQs who fail to achieve success in life because they lacked self-discipline and of people of low IQs who succeeded by virtue of persistence, reliability and self-discipline. Heckman and Rubinstein (2001b), p. 145

While cognitive ability reflects what an individual can do, it is non-cognitive factors that reflect what an individual will do. McGeown et al. (2015), p. 12

Good character education is good education ... we need to take character education as seriously as we take academic education. Berkowitz and Bier (2005), p. 3

Past Performance, Future Performance

About ten years ago, we had an epiphany of sorts. We were working together leading a comprehensive school sixth form in Greater Manchester, desperate to lift pupil performance and further strengthen the learning culture we had inherited. Analysing that particular summer's results, something seemed suddenly clear. There didn't seem to be a direct link between success at the end of one key stage and success at the next. Checking off those results learner by learner, it was obvious that some made giant strides between 16 and 18, leaping up from pretty modest results at the end of Key Stage 4 to outstanding results in Key Stage 5, while others went from great performance at 16 to modest grades at the end of their A level courses.

Why was this? We drew up a list of all the factors we considered might play a part in these deviations from expectation. Some were external (illness, family issues, mental health issues), some were behavioural (disengagement, listlessness, lack of effort) and some were psychological (lack of belief, deeply entrenched pessimism). It might have ended there, but that autumn term we began to study what it was about the 'ceiling pupils' that made them stop progressing and what it was about the 'breakthrough pupils' that made them suddenly improve. We identified

sample groups, handed out questionnaires, observed kids during lessons, evaluated previous academic performance and took part in focus groups. We met the pupils regularly and talked about their approaches to study.

Put simply, we'd stumbled across the role that non-cognitive factors play in successful learning: the fact that *past performance didn't guarantee future performance*. This ran counter to what some of our colleagues were telling us, and indeed what we'd thought ourselves at various stages of our careers. Listen for explanations of pupil underperformance at your place of work and the chances are they'll be mostly cognitive and often inextricably linked to previous performance; rooted in a sense of inevitability that the past equals the future. You might hear that the pupil 'has always been weak', they were from a 'lower set', they 'didn't get it', they were going to find their GCSE courses 'too hard', they've 'never been a natural scientist', we 'shouldn't expect too much of them' and they've 'always struggled with languages'.

Catch-all explanations like these externally justify pupil performance – they get the grades they do for reasons beyond a teacher's control – and seem, to us at least, to remove responsibility for encouraging any further progress. 'Give me some decent kids', one member of staff once told us, 'and I'll give you some decent results.'

But we were seeing something very different. We were seeing a range of attitudes, values and mental models which accreted to form a set of behaviours that, in turn, determined the way in which pupils approached their studies.

Here's just one study to consider – there are plenty more on the way. Mike Treadaway at research group Education Datalab has completed a fascinating study into pupil progress across different key stages. His findings are initially shocking but, on reflection, predictable. 'We have an accountability system that has encouraged schools to check that children are making a certain number of sub-levels of progress each year,' Treadaway begins in his 2015 paper, 'Why measuring pupil progress involves more than taking a straight line'. He explains: 'Take a child's attainment at Key Stage One (age 7), look up the average attainment for children at the same level by Key Stage Two (age 11) and draw a straight line between the two assuming that linear progress will be made in each of the four intervening years.' The same happens between Key Stages 3 and 4, of course, and then 4 and 5; the past equals the future. 'But,' Treadaway asks, 'do children normally take such smooth learning journeys as they acquire knowledge and understanding in a subject as our accountability system assumes? And is it reasonable to deem children as "on target" or "in need of intervention" using this approach?'

The findings are alarming. Treadaway notes that 'by reviewing the data we find that only 9% of pupils take the expected pathways through Key Stage Two, Key Stage Three and Key Stage Four Levels'. Less than one in ten pupils follow the line we're using to anticipate and measure their progress. That's across three key stages, you might think – shorten the period of time and huge numbers of kids will turn out to be on the line. Well, the figure goes up, sure. But nowhere near as much as you might expect. Performance at point A – wherever you choose that to be – doesn't guarantee performance at point B, just as we'd found.

So where *are* the 91% of pupils who should be on the line? And why aren't they there? Well, some are above it and some are below it, just like our initial metaphor of the 'ceiling' pupils and the 'breakthrough' pupils. As to why, when we stopped using previous performance as an indicator of likely future success and analysed instead our ceiling pupils' habits, routines, attitudes and approaches to study, that's when we found patterns. Here are a few examples of the kind of similarities we discovered. Detailed note-taking seemed to be a characteristic of those who left the line upwards. Tidiness and organisation of learning resources seemed important too, as were acknowledging and working on weaknesses. Commitment to independent study was key. Positivity, enthusiasm and having a goal all came through as characteristics and behaviours that breakthrough pupils had and did a lot of, and ceiling pupils didn't.

It was, and continues to be in our experience, *skills*, *strategies* and *habitualised behaviours* that determined academic success. These can change, and pupils can leave the line as a result. Damaging attitudes and beliefs can become entrenched, levels of effort can vary, commitment falters and organisational systems collapse under the pressure of a new key stage.

Performance Virtues

The discussion around developing pupils' non-cognitive skills has continued to be high on the agenda for practitioners, school leaders and governments. But attempting to develop these non-cognitive skills and habits without knowing precisely what they are is nigh on impossible. So how do we categorise and define these characteristics? And what language do we use while we attempt to do so?

Perhaps one of the most significant developments in the last few years has been the work of the Jubilee Centre for Character and Virtues at the University of Birmingham. (We would strongly recommend all readers to visit www.jubileecentre.ac.uk and take advantage of the extensive resources that

they offer – it's a treasure trove.) The Jubilee Centre defines these non-cognitive qualities as 'a set of personal traits and dispositions that produces specific moral emotions, informs motivation and guides conduct' (Jubilee Centre for Character and Virtues, 2017, p. 2), and their research identifies four categories that they refer to as 'virtues':

» Intellectual virtues such as curiosity and critical thinking.

» Moral virtues such as courage, honesty, humility, empathy and gratitude.

» Civic virtues such as acts of service and volunteering.

» Performance virtues such as resilience, application and self-regulation.

We believe that this framework provides a really useful starting point when considering the virtues and characteristics that any school would want to develop in their pupils. The Jubilee Centre makes a compelling argument that schools should consider intellectual, moral, civic and performance virtues when considering the kind of citizens it wants to develop (Figure 0.1).

We were lucky. When we began this work we were operating in a school whose pastoral systems and structures were geared towards outstanding delivery of moral and civic virtues. And, as Figure 0.2 illustrates, civic and moral virtues are strongly connected

Figure 0.1. Non-cognitive qualities: the building blocks

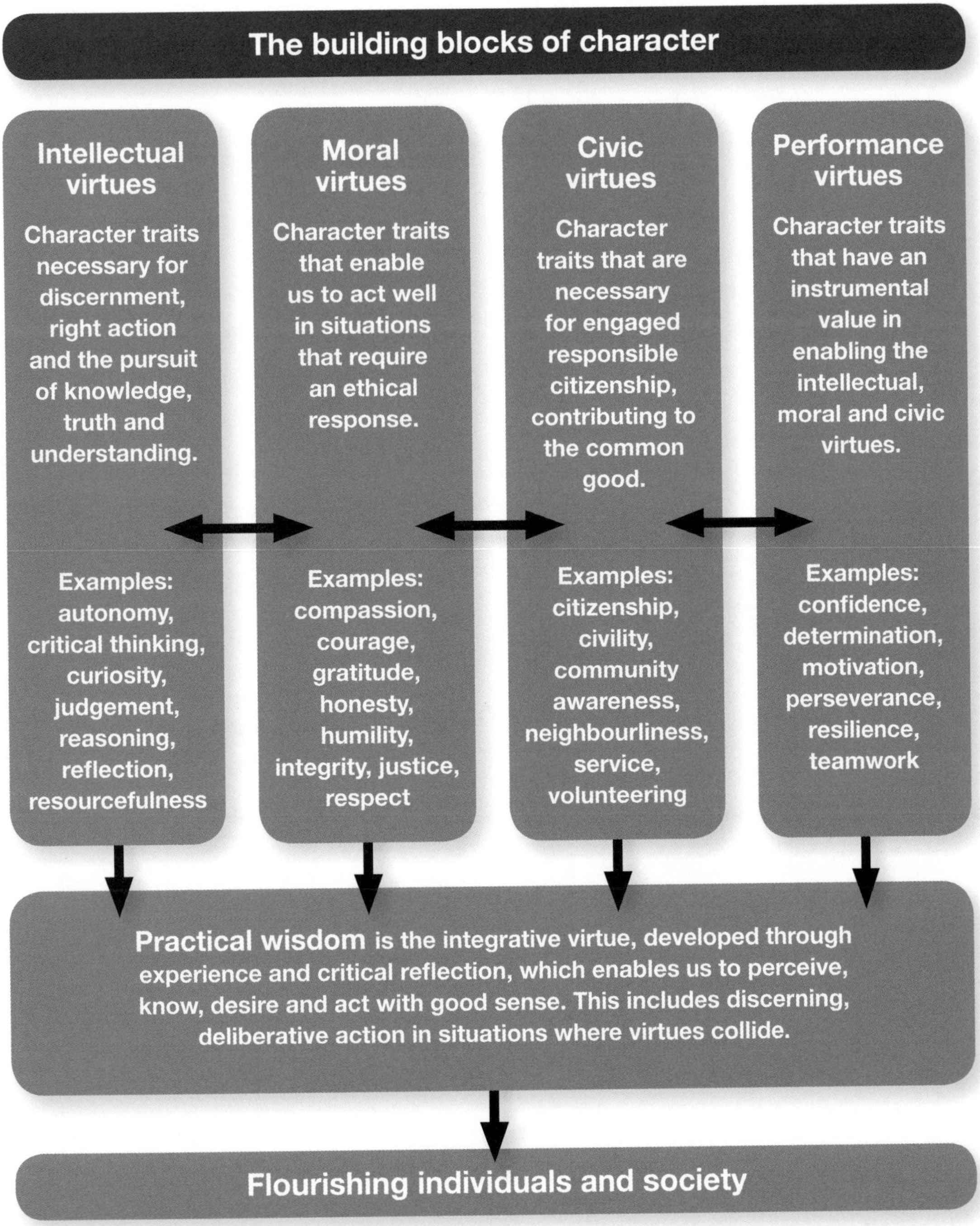

The building blocks of character

Intellectual virtues	Moral virtues	Civic virtues	Performance virtues
Character traits necessary for discernment, right action and the pursuit of knowledge, truth and understanding.	Character traits that enable us to act well in situations that require an ethical response.	Character traits that are necessary for engaged responsible citizenship, contributing to the common good.	Character traits that have an instrumental value in enabling the intellectual, moral and civic virtues.
Examples: autonomy, critical thinking, curiosity, judgement, reasoning, reflection, resourcefulness	Examples: compassion, courage, gratitude, honesty, humility, integrity, justice, respect	Examples: citizenship, civility, community awareness, neighbourliness, service, volunteering	Examples: confidence, determination, motivation, perseverance, resilience, teamwork

Practical wisdom is the integrative virtue, developed through experience and critical reflection, which enables us to perceive, know, desire and act with good sense. This includes discerning, deliberative action in situations where virtues collide.

Flourishing individuals and society

Source: Jubilee Centre for Character and Virtues (2017), p. 5.

to academic performance and develop academic behaviours that are important in the classroom. We were at an advantage.

Knowing the school operated extremely well in terms of the development of civic and moral virtues, and that we were doubtless experiencing a positive knock-on effect of the sort illustrated here, we found our attention focused on *performance virtues* – the business of making pupils better learners.

Figure 0.2. Linking virtues to academic performance

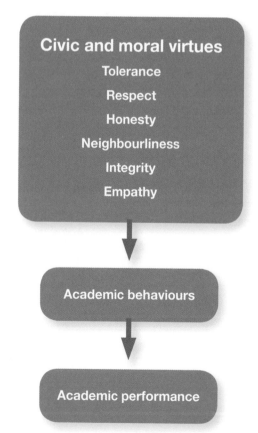

This choice emerged from our context and circumstances. We didn't know it at the time but the argument for developing pupils' performance virtues has continued to gain momentum (see Gutman and Schoon, 2013 for a review).

Non-Cognitive Skills and Seven Crucial Constructs

> Achievement tests miss, or perhaps more accurately, do not adequately capture, soft skills – personality traits, goals, motivations, and preferences – that are valued in the labor market, in school, and in many other domains.
>
> Heckman and Kautz (2012), p. 451

The terms used – the language of performance virtues, if you like – continue to generate considerable debate. If you're interested in researching and reading further, you might find performance virtues variously described as non-cognitive skills, soft skills, twenty-first century skills, character skills, and social and emotional learning skills.

There are advantages and disadvantages to all of these terms, but the easiest to conceive of and consider, for us, has been 'non-cognitive skills'. Whatever your preference or inclination, the most important thing, of course, is the universal use of the term 'skills', which suggests a series of approaches, strategies and tools that can be learned.

So what are these essential skills, exactly? And which ones should we prioritise?

There is, as you might imagine, considerable discussion over this. Go looking for a universal measure of non-cognitive skills and you'll be disappointed. Instead, you'll find a large range of models or 'constructs' used to describe and explain non-cognitive skills, offered up by a huge number of academics and researchers from a vast array of institutions. There's a lot of noise out there.

We've studied pretty much all of them, and tried to distil the best of them for you here. Think of this section of the book as a sort of crash course in the role of non-cognitive skills in academic performance, and you won't go far wrong. We've identified seven constructs (see Figure 0.3) which we think are key to pupil success. We're going to refer to these in subsequent chapters so they deserve some explanation here. Some of them will be familiar – apologies for rehashing; others hopefully less so.

Figure 0.3. Seven important non-cognitive constructs in education

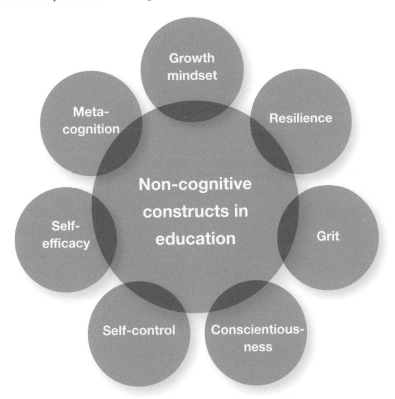

Growth Mindset

Most teachers are now familiar with the work of Carol Dweck (2017). If not, we would strongly recommend her book, *Mindset: Changing the Way You Think to Fulfil Your Potential*. Her research suggests that beliefs about ability and intelligence vary greatly, and that the beliefs adopted by a young person can have a significant impact on their achievements. She argues that individuals have a certain 'mindset' regarding their ability, and that this mindset is a fluid and changing thing. At one end of the continuum are those who believe they have a 'fixed' mindset. These individuals suppose that their intelligence is fixed at a certain point and, as a result, avoid challenging situations because they fear failure. They withdraw effort during difficult tasks to protect their ego.

At the other end of the continuum are those with a 'growth' mindset. These individuals believe that intelligence is malleable and that if you work hard you can improve your level of ability. They put themselves in challenging situations and work their way through them, listening to feedback and acting on it. They view failure as an opportunity to grow and, as a result, behave in a very different way in a learning environment. In other words, the two types of pupil operate differently, study differently and think differently.

Dweck goes on to say that our mindset changes in response to challenge, growth or circumstance. 'Nobody has a growth mindset in everything all the time,' Dweck notes. 'Everyone is a mixture of fixed and growth mindsets. You could have a predominant growth mindset in an area but there can still be things that trigger you into a fixed mindset trait' (see Gross-Loh, 2016).

We've found Dweck's work to be extremely valuable, and it's certainly helped to shape our thinking. A pupil's mindset – a snapshot, at least, of a fluid mindset – can be measured using Dweck's mindset questionnaire: https://mindsetonline.com/testyourmindset/step1.php. There is some evidence to show that a pupil's growth mindset links to academic performance and that it can be developed (Yeager et al., 2013).

Grit

Angela Duckworth's work on grit has gained a lot of media attention since her 2013 TED Talk (which is worth watching if you're new to grit). Duckworth (2016) defines grit as an individual's passion and perseverance towards long-term goals. What distinguishes grit from some of the other constructs discussed here is its reference to long-term goals. Duckworth argues that maintaining effort and interest over the years, despite setbacks, are the main characteristics of the gritty individual.

We believe that GCSEs require pupils to be gritty. Grit can be measured using the grit scale developed by Duckworth and her colleagues (2007). We've included the questionnaire as one of the tools in Chapter 4. Duckworth has recently set up a lab to focus on how to intentionally cultivate grit. Her website (https://characterlab.org/tools/grit) offers a range of tools that can be used with pupils.

Self-efficacy

Self-efficacy is an individual's belief that they have the capability to succeed at a particular task. Most teachers will have had experience of working with pupils who have faced repeated failure and as a result have low self-efficacy. It seems obvious with these pupils that if we get them to succeed (even on a small scale), then their confidence and motivation should increase.

There is a reasonable amount of evidence to show that pupils with high self-efficacy work harder and persevere more (Multon et al., 1991) and there is some solid evidence that it is a useful predictor of academic success (Bandura, 1997). A number of scales are used to measure self-efficacy – for example, the Motivated Strategies for Learning Questionnaire shows evidence of high levels of reliability and validity.* There are a few studies that have attempted to develop pupils' self-efficacy (e.g. Schunk, 1981);

however, most of the studies that have been undertaken have simply shown a correlation between the construct and academic performance.

Conscientiousness

Conscientiousness is part of the 'big-five' personality model (a famous model developed over a century or so ago, with Lewis Goldberg coining the term as part of his contribution in the 1980s) which suggests that there are five broad dimensions to personality: openness to experience, conscientiousness, extraversion, agreeableness and neuroticism. Conscientiousness is the most widely predictive of the commonly used personality measures. It has been linked to academic performance at all levels of schooling (Poropat, 2009) and studies show that it predicts 'educational attainment, health, and labor market outcomes as strongly as measures of cognitive ability' (Heckman and Kautz, 2012, p. 452).

Personality inventories define a range of lower level traits that sit under conscientiousness; however (surprise!), there is some disagreement about which traits. The two most common are orderliness and industriousness. Orderliness does what it says on the tin – organisation, in other words – and industriousness describes a predisposition

---

* See http://stelar.edc.org/instruments/motivated-strategies-learning-questionnaire-mslq.

for hard work and persistence (Ivcevic and Brackett, 2014).

There are a number of measures used to evaluate the 'big five' personality traits (e.g. the Big Five Inventory which can be found online*). Like self-efficacy, most of the studies on conscientiousness are correlational. To date, there has been very little research undertaken on attempting to develop conscientiousness in pupils, partly due to the complexity of this interrelated construct.

Self-control

Self-control, which is generally defined 'as the ability to resist short-term impulses in order to prioritise longer-term goals' (Gutman and Schoon, 2013, p. 20), is considered to be a lower level trait or facet of conscientiousness.

Perhaps the most famous study testing self-control is the 'marshmallow experiment', conducted by Mischel et al. (1972) at Stanford University, which has since become a school assembly classic. Most teachers and pupils have now watched the video clips of young children being given a marshmallow and then offered a reward if they are able to delay gratification. In follow-up studies, pupils who were able to wait (around fifteen minutes) were found to do better academically and had better life outcomes.

Apart from doing the marshmallow test in class, the self-control scale developed by Tangney and colleagues (2004) is probably the most widely used (pupils might prefer the thirteen-item version to the ninety-three items!). Despite strong correlational evidence suggesting that self-control predicts academic outcomes, there have been few studies that have attempted to develop self-control in isolation. We've found, like many of you, that showing videos related to the marshmallow experiment can generate some interesting discussions with pupils, but we have struggled to design specific tools to develop this particular trait (though Now vs. Most (Activity 36) has a pretty good stab at it).

Resilience and Buoyancy

Resilience is a term that we are hearing a lot on our visits to schools. Resilience has typically been characterised 'in terms of "acute" and "chronic" adversities that are seen as "major assaults" on the developmental processes' (Martin and Marsh, 2008, p. 53).

We prefer the term suggested by Martin and Marsh, which is 'academic buoyancy'. In the classroom it's more about bouncing back from small disappointments and setbacks rather than acute or chronic adversities. We appreciate that resilience might be needed by some pupils who have these types of events in their lives, but not by the majority.

* See http://personality-testing.info/tests/IPIP-BFFM/.

There are a number of organisations using a resilience framework to support the development of young people. Professor Angie Hart at the University of Brighton probably leads this field of work in the UK. Her website (www.boingboing.org.uk) supplies an overview of the framework and a much more thorough explanation of resilience than we've provided here.

Meta-cognition

Finally, meta-cognition was a term initially developed by Flavell (1979). He referred to it as 'thinking about thinking'. We have saved this term until last since, for us, meta-cognition encapsulates elements of all the constructs discussed above. The term has now been broadened quite significantly and is used regularly. The Education Endowment Foundation (EEF), for example, suggest that it's about helping 'learners think about their own learning more explicitly. This is usually by teaching pupils specific strategies to set goals, and monitor and evaluate their own academic development.'*

There are a number of inventories/ questionnaires used to measure meta-cognition (including our own in Chapter 13), and a range of interesting research projects currently being delivered in the UK that are using meta-cognitive strategies to support and improve pupil performance. It's worth visiting the EEF website to check on their progress; we will be.

As you can see, it's a complicated world of research, conjecture and experimentation out there!

What seems to be beyond doubt is that non-cognitive skills contribute significantly to pupils' performance; the evidence base for this is convincing and is growing considerably (e.g. Khine and Areepattamannil, 2016). It's notable that, as courses lose their modular elements, non-cognitive skills become even more important; a pupil's grit, self-belief, self-control and resilience become significant factors as the period of pre-exam preparation extends and performance is judged by a single terminal exam. The short-term snapshots of monthly test scores, for example, tell us one thing; the final exam tells us quite another. Farrington et al. (2012) illustrate this well, and provide a useful visual summary of where non-cognitive factors fit over the distance of a two-year qualification (Figure 0.4).

---

* See https://educationendowmentfoundation.org.uk/resources/teaching-learning-toolkit/meta-cognition-and-self-regulation/.

Figure 0.4. Factors measured by test scores vs. grades

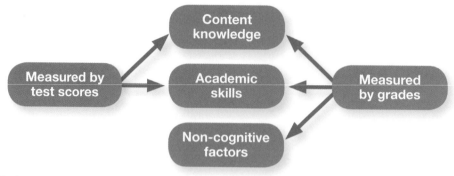

Source: Farrington et al. (2012), p. 4.

(It's worth noting that, to date, there is no conclusive evidence on the percentage distribution of these factors.)

We hope that, like us, you're getting to grips with the possible components we need to be strengthening and developing in our pupils. Next, it's time to turn our attention to the rest of the book: the 'how'.

Practical Tools and Strategies – The 'How' of Non-Cognitive Skills Development

> For all the discussion of non-cognitive factors in recent years, there has been little conclusive agreement on how best to help young people develop them.
>
> Tough (2016), p. 5

Awareness of non-cognitive factors, and of their importance, has been with us for a long time. Alfred Binet and his collaborator, Theodore Simon – the French psychologists responsible for the invention of the IQ test – were considering non-cognitive factors in 1916, when they suggested: '[Success in school] … admits of other things than intelligence; to succeed in his studies, one must have qualities which depend on attention, will, and character; for example a certain docility, a regularity of habits, and especially continuity of effort. A child, even if intelligent, will learn little in class if he never listens, if he spends his time in playing tricks, in giggling, in playing truant' (Binet and Simon, 1916, p. 254).

Looked at from this perspective, progress in the academic world around developing non-cognitive skills in young learners has been frustratingly slow. If Binet and Simon could see us now, a hundred years later, they would surely be sorely disappointed with education's lack of progress in this area.

So, why has it been so hard to make progress?

Two reasons, we think. First, much of the conflicting research between many of the theoretical models and constructs (operationalised by an array of inventories) has left us all a little confused. There's just so much out there, and no unifying theory. (See the Authors' Note at the beginning of the book for a short summary of information abundance and paralysis.)

A second frustration has been that most of the research can be pretty inaccessible to teachers on both a practical and academic level. Very few of the academic papers we've been discussing offer any real practical suggestions to the profession. (We share the sentiments of the *British Medical Journal*, which has now banned the phrase 'more research is needed'! More research is always needed, but at some point we have to look at how the theory can be put into practice.) We've found that many school leaders and teachers are unsure how to make the leap from theory to practice – beyond telling pupils about the studies, that is – and unsure how to develop these important skills with their pupils in a coaching or classroom environment. There is a danger that, because of these difficulties, the evident advantages to teaching non-cognitive skills will just get ignored.

Since the publication of *The A Level Mindset* we've been overwhelmed with the positive responses the book has received from practitioners. As we've travelled up and down the country visiting schools and colleges delivering training on the VESPA model (more on this later) teachers have been asking us, 'How can we deliver this to GCSE pupils?' We've been asked continually for practical tools and strategies that might make a difference to pupils at Key Stage 4.

The remainder of this book concerns itself, therefore, with the 'how' of non-cognitive skills development – with turning theory into concrete practice. Rather than align ourselves too closely with any one particular model or construct, we've tried to incorporate the most relevant and useful constructs from all the research we've read into one simple framework that can be used practically with teachers and pupils. We'll share that with you in the next chapter.*

In developing our model and tools, we've tried to make sense of the research and develop a practical approach that can, hopefully, be used by teachers in their classrooms and have an impact on their pupils' performance, developing strategies, habits and skills that will be useful beyond the classroom.

This is our attempt at imposing some sort of order on the chaos.

---

* We're aware of the irony here. The problem is too many models so our solution is another model. Ridiculous, right? Our hope, though, is that this is less a set of new propositions and theories in non-cognitive skills, and more a unifying theory that organises existing research in an accessible and actionable way.

1. The VESPA Model

An Introduction to VESPA

Our work, undertaken across both Key Stage 4 and 5 over the last eight years, suggests that a five-part model is at the heart of non-cognitive skill development and academic success. Each part is as important as the others.

Pupils who are successful score highly in the following qualities:

» **Vision** – they know what they want to achieve.

» **Effort** – they work hard and put in many hours of proactive independent study.

» **Systems** – they organise their learning resources and their time.

» **Practice** – they use deliberate practice and develop their skills.

» **Attitude** – they have a growth mindset and respond constructively to setbacks.

Why these five qualities?

For us, the VESPA model emerged as the best fit to explain the myriad of non-cognitive attributes we were trying to make sense of as we spoke to pupils, designed interventions, built pastoral programmes and read academic research. We didn't start with the traditional approach of looking at the research and trying to fit our data into a pre-established model. We also didn't use any psychometric measures. We simply collected data on our own pupils through lesson observations, focus groups, questionnaires and coaching conversations; a whole bunch of quantitative and qualitative data with analysis. (It was only later that we discovered that we'd used what academics call a 'ground theory approach'. First published in Glaser and Strauss' *The Discovery of Grounded Theory* (1967), it suggests that you collect data and then try to make sense of it by categorising the findings yourself, rather than beginning with the literature and making the data fit a pre-established model. We reviewed the literature once we'd designed the model, rather than the other way around.)

Soon after building the VESPA model it became pretty obvious to us that we hadn't stumbled across anything new, we'd just developed a multidimensional 'umbrella' (Figure 1.1b) that seemed to incorporate many of the constructs being discussed. We were going for actionable and workable – a simple, visual summary of the non-cognitive factors we wanted to focus on, with a set of tools for strengthening those qualities. It was by coincidence that we later discovered we supported the view of the Education Endowment Foundation that 'Many of the non-cognitive factors are inter-linked, yet most studies examine non-cognitive skills in isolation. There is no conclusive evidence which of the diverse characteristics is the one crucial "silver bullet" to improve or facilitate attainment across all domains, and it is unlikely that such a characteristic can be found' (Gutman and Schoon, 2013, p. 4).

We don't have any hard evidence to support this precise hierarchical organisation (as the EEF suggest, there's no evidence of a silver bullet). The relationship between these factors is, no doubt, a lot more complex than we've suggested. That said, for us, vision is key. First, you have to know why you are doing something. Next, you must have the right attitude towards the task. Effort, systems and practice can all be applied to the vision.

Over the years of testing, experimenting and using we've helped thousands of pupils to perform better at Key Stages 4 and 5 by:

» Building pastoral programmes which explicitly focus on developing these non-cognitive skills.

» Designing a coaching framework which focuses on VESPA.

Figure 1.1a. The VESPA model

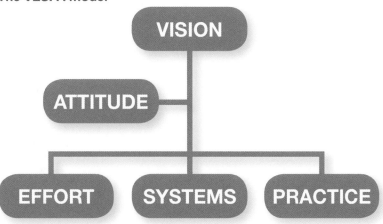

Figure 1.1b. The VESPA umbrella

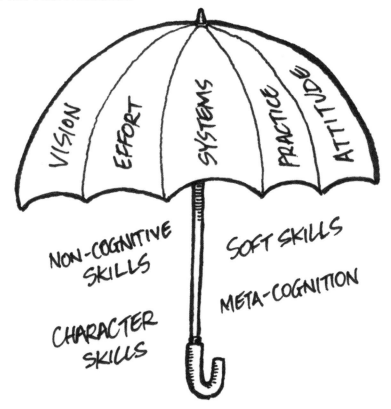

The VESPA Model

Vision

← →

May resent setting goals and targets	Likes setting goals and targets
Unlikely to set goals for themselves	Often sets personal bests to measure themselves against
Has no real purpose	Has a clear purpose in life

Effort

← →

Avoids hard work	Knows what hard work looks like
Compares effort to other low effort pupils	Surrounds themselves with other hard working pupils
Easily distracted	Totally focused when working

Systems

← →

Has completely disorganised books and notes (if they have them at all!)	Has organised books and notes
Has no record of tasks or homework	Records homework in planner or diary
Works reactively in response to crisis	Plans their work appropriately

Practice

← →

Relies on reading notes and highlighters for revision	Uses a range of techniques when revising
Most of their time is spent on work they already know	Looks for opportunities to work outside of their comfort zone
Avoids feedback	Always seeking feedback on performance

Attitude

← →

Believes that intelligence is fixed	Believes that if you work hard you can improve your level of ability
Responds poorly to feedback	Believes feedback will make them better
Low levels of self-control	Stays calm in high stakes situations
Lacks confidence	High levels of self-belief

» Designing intervention programmes that target deficiencies in non-cognitive skills through VESPA, rather than assume an issue with understanding or comprehension.

It might be worth taking a moment to consider the model from your own perspective and context, by considering particular groups of underperforming or high performing pupils, and running a mental checklist against the continua we've produced on page 18. For the purposes of emphasis and contrast we've used descriptors associated with the more extreme positions at either ends of the spectrum. Hopefully, these will clarify what we mean by each skill area and help you to begin to explore the kinds of characteristics associated with high or low vision, effort, systems, practice or attitude.

One more thing. It's worth pointing out – as Dweck herself has noted – that mindset is a fluid thing. Try to avoid the trap of concluding a student is 'high vision' and assuming that to be a permanent and unchanging state of being. Our mindsets change in response to developing external and internal circumstances.

Research Supporting the VESPA Model

We've been lucky that there has been some high quality research under each element of the VESPA model. This research has been undertaken by some of the most prolific researchers in psychology and education. Any teacher or leader working long hours with limited opportunity to dig in to academic journals and papers can find it difficult to know where to begin, so here are useful some starting points.

On Vision

Vision is about having a clear goal; it's about making the connection between the work you are doing and the reason for doing it. It's also about setting yourself targets for improvement. In simple terms, it's about knowing the outcomes you want to achieve. Duckworth (2016) emphasises 'stickability' to a long-term goal, but we've found making goals shorter term works well for low vision pupils. If they can't tell you where they want to be when they're 18, for example, try 'Your next report goes home in four weeks. What grades would you like to see on that report? How can we go about making that happen?'

Of course, simply setting goals doesn't necessarily improve achievement (Schunk, 2003). If only it were that simple! There are three parts to vision.

Step 1 is deciding what you want to achieve. This doesn't have to be about identifying a specific career path, as we discuss later (see Chapter 3). For some pupils, it can involve assessing motivators and drivers, considering problems and issues they'd like to help solve or something as simple as deciding on some of the outcomes they'd like to achieve.

Step 2 is the goal setting process you put in place to achieve the vision. Most goal setting stops at step 1. Pupils write down their goals and then don't design a specific plan to make them happen. Duckworth (2016, p. 62) suggests that we envision a hierarchy of low, mid and top level goals (Figure 1.2).

The top level goal is the ultimate concern. The mid and lower level goals are merely a list of tasks that need to be completed to achieve that goal. For example, a pupil might have an ultimate goal of 'contributing to improving healthcare in the UK'. Underneath that are a number of mid and low level goals that will help them to achieve that. A mid level goal could be to visit a potential university, but to make that happen several low level goals might need to be completed. This is a really effective process of goal setting and provides the pupil with a ready-made checklist that has the potential to become a visual goal setting tool.

Step 3 is about sticking to the plan – what Duckworth (2016) calls grit. This can be the tricky bit. It involves reflecting on the progress being made towards goals and making any

Figure 1.2. Low, mid and top level goals

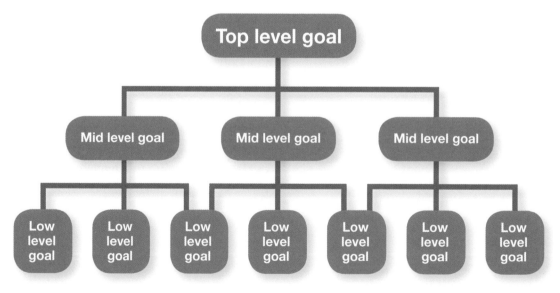

Source: Adapted from Duckworth (2016), p. 62.

Figure 1.3. The goal setting process

necessary adjustments. As discussed earlier, grit is about having the top level goal for a long time. The complete process is illustrated in Figure 1.3.

The goal can then be made SMART. Most teachers are now familiar with the acronym that describes the goal setting process: goals should be *specific*, *measurable*, *achievable*, *relevant* and *time-bound*.

There are a number of studies that show goal setting enhances achievement (Moriarity et al., 2001). These studies have included both long-term and short-term goals. There is also evidence to show that pupils should be involved in setting their own goals (Azevedo et al., 2002). Externally imposed goals do little for motivation (just ask most teachers about how they feel when given targets).

In the past, we've used the terms 'push' and 'pull' goals. A push goal is externally imposed and is used to push you towards an objective. Push goals are usually only as strong as the person doing the pushing, and if they are met with resistance they often fail. A pull goal is self-imposed and therefore (in theory) makes it more likely that the individual will be motivated to follow through. According to the Prince's Trust, there is an argument that we are guilty of doing too much pushing through the GCSE years and that this takes away the future-mindedness of the pupil and makes them feel that they have a lack of control over their life.*

Throughout the book, the vision activities have been designed to help support pupils on this element. We would strongly recommend that every school should know who their low vision pupils are and have an action plan to help move them along this scale from September.

On Effort

The effort (sometimes called academic perseverance) element of the VESPA model refers to how much hard work you do; performance on most tasks depends on effort (Heckman and Kautz, 2012). It's probably fair to say that the absence of effort pretty much guarantees failure; however, more effort on its own is not a guarantee of success! You obviously have to practise in the right way (more on this later).

This issue has caused some considerable debate recently due to the claims made by Malcolm Gladwell in his book *Outliers* (2008) regarding the 10,000 hour rule. Gladwell suggests that elite performers will generally have put in 10,000 hours of work to become the best in any field. However, Anders Ericsson and Robert Pool (2016), who did the initial research used in Gladwell's book, claim that Gladwell misinterpreted the research in a number of ways. First, effort varies from field to field. In music, for example, many top musicians quite often exceed this number of hours, whereas Ericsson found that you could become a world memory champion in far fewer hours. Second, Gladwell used the average hours of practice that violin pupils had put in by the time they were 20, but Ericsson claims that most weren't top performers by this age. However, one thing both Gladwell and Ericsson do agree on is that 'becoming accomplished in any field in which there is a well-established history of people working to become experts requires a tremendous amount of effort exerted over many years. It may not be 10,000, but it will take a lot' (Ericsson and Pool, 2016, p. 112).

Perhaps one of the most useful ways of thinking about the importance of effort has been presented by Angela Duckworth (2016, p. 42). She has provided an equation that is useful for thinking about effort and sharing with your pupils! She suggests the following:

---

* See https://www.princes-trust.org.uk/about-the-trust/research-policies-reports/youth-index-2017.

Talent x Effort = Skill

Skill x Effort = Achievement

Talent, she claims, is how quickly your skills improve when you invest effort. Achievement is when you take your acquired skills and use them. What's most interesting about this equation is that effort factors twice in the equation!

Our research found that there was a link between effort and achievement. In *The A Level Mindset* (2016, p. 41) we introduced the 1–10 scale, and it's worth mentioning again here as it's the key to explaining effort to your pupils. In order to effectively measure, encourage and model high levels of effort, first you have to quantify it in a way that unifies everyone's thinking and in a way that everyone can understand. We've worked with

a lot of schools that report on pupil effort to parents; however, when teachers are asked to quantify this they usually have very different responses. The effort message transmitted to pupils can be quite confusing. In our research, we started by asking pupils how hard they thought they were working on a 1–10 scale. We used the following guidelines to help pupils with their thinking:

» **1** – Little or no effort

» **5** – Some effort – you're working quite hard

» **10** – High levels of effort – the hardest you've worked

You can probably guess what the typical response was: most pupils said, 'About a 6, Sir'. We soon realised that this was a pointless exercise; how a pupil rates their effort will quite often depend on their own reference bias (Duckworth and Yeager, 2015). A 'frame of reference' means that individuals generally judge their performance based on the people they are surrounded

On a scale of one to ten

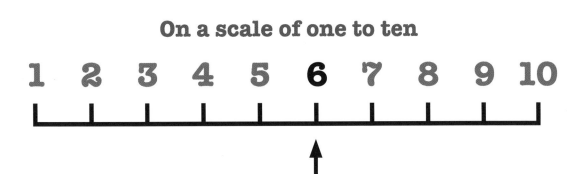

by. We found that the main problems with reference bias are:

» The numbers mean different things to different people.

» Pupils tend to surround themselves with peers who do either similar or less work than they do. This means they 'normalise' the amount of work they are doing, even feel good about it, because they can point to someone doing less than they are.

» Pupils don't have a clear idea of what the hardest working pupils are doing.

» No one can know what pupils are doing in other schools.

We decided to collect data on how much effort (hours of independent work) pupils were putting in at certain points of the year. When we did our research we were looking at Year 12 pupils. We collected the data through questionnaires over a few years. We found that pupils at the lower end of the scale were doing about 0–2 hours of independent study a week and at the top of the scale they were doing about 20 hours per week (from about March onwards).

» **1:** 0–2 hours independent study a week

» **5:** 10 hours independent study a week

» **10:** 20 hours independent study a week

This provided us and the pupils with a useful reference point. We could measure effort, to some extent. It also became clear that pupils who were getting better grades were putting more effort into their studies. Of course, there were pupils putting the effort in and not getting good grades; quite often they were practising in the wrong way.

Do you know how many hours of independent work your top GCSE pupils are doing each week? If not, we would strongly recommend you do this exercise in your school.

Measuring effort can be quite tricky. There are other ways, such as measuring specific time 'on task' (without losing focus) that pupils spend in lessons or looking at the quality and quantity of homework pupils produce. Perhaps one of the most important messages to transmit to your pupils is the 'myth of effortless success'. Pupils only get to fully understand this when they see and hear the amount of effort that has generally gone into a successful performance.

In summary, there has been limited research on the level (or amount) of effort related to pupils' exam performance (Jung et al., 2016). Some studies in the United States have found that study time per week was positively related to grade point average (Strauss and Volkwein, 2002). In our small scale study, the relationship between effort and academic performance was very clear; however, we appreciate that some teachers may prefer the term 'efficient effort' (developed by Jung et al., 2016). They suggest that efficient effort is the time pupils spend on a task in such a way that their return on investment is maximised. For us this means:

Effort x Practice = Efficient return on investment

On Systems

Systems is about two things: (1) a system to organise learning so pupils can make sense of it all and (2) a system to organise their time so pupils can complete key tasks to deadlines. We find this definition of systems much more helpful than the nebulous term 'study skills', which is tricky to define and serves to make the whole process seem more complex than it is.

The importance of good systems is often overlooked – Hassanbeigi and colleagues (2011, p. 1418) even suggest that 'for many pupils, academic challenges are related more to a lack of organisation than to a lack of intellectual ability'. Hassanbeigi's research looked at systems used by university students using something researchers referred to as a Study Skills Assessment Questionnaire. The questionnaire was developed by counselling services at Houston University and examines a number of areas including: time management, procrastination and organising and processing information. Their sample

consisted of 179 male pupils. They found that pupils with a higher grade point average were statistically higher in all of the following skills: note-taking, organising information and time management.

It's only one study; however, it would be interesting to look at the relationship between GCSE grades and systems. We've often found a clear link between pupils who are underperforming and poor organisation and project management. The time spent on developing these skills has a significant return on investment, so we've included a number of tools to help improve these habits in GCSE pupils.

On Practice

We see practice as distinct from effort – it represents what learners do with the time they put into their studies. Not the 'how much' of study but the 'how'.

Tom Stafford and Michael Dewar (2014) found that when it comes to learning quickly, it's the way you practise and not how often you practise that counts. They analysed data from 854,064 players on an online game looking at how practice affected subsequent performances. Practice doesn't make perfect; deliberate practice makes perfect. In other words, effort alone is not enough to guarantee success. Academic progress is as much about how you work as it is about how long you work for. Pupils who are putting in large amounts of time and effort but not making progress, are very often working on the wrong things.

It's hard to talk about practice without mentioning the work of Anders Ericsson. Ericsson has spent his entire career looking at top level performers in a number of fields. His conclusion is that top performers don't just practise hard, they practise in a particular way. He calls this 'deliberate practice' and suggests there are some key principles that are needed to enter this type of practice:

1 A clearly defined stretch goal. This has to be very specific and measurable. For example, if a pupil was doing a past GCSE paper they might select all the questions they found difficult and attempt these within a specific time frame. It's the 'stretch' aspect that's key. You have to practise outside your comfort zone.

2 Full concentration and effort. Ericsson argues that deliberate practice is quite often done individually. This prevents distractions.

3 Immediate and informative feedback. This can be tricky for GCSE pupils, but they should seek feedback as close as possible to their performance.

4 Deliberate practice requires repetition with reflection and refinement. For example, as soon as a pupil realises they have made mistakes (immediately after stage 3), they must go back and correct their work.

How many pupils do you know who practise in this way? Most revision techniques used by pupils never enter deliberate practice. Reading through notes and highlighting key terms doesn't even get you to stage 1! We think that understanding practice is key to pupils' performance, and we will share with you the revision questionnaire (Chapter 6) to help you identify how pupils might be practising.

On Attitude

We believe there are four elements to developing pupils' attitude (in relation to performance virtues). These are confidence (in particular confidence in abilities), emotional control, academic buoyancy and growth mindset (see Figure 1.4).

Confidence is key to academic success (Stankov and Lee, 2014). We have tried to include a number of tools in the book that help to build pupils' confidence. It can be a slow process and involves small

Figure 1.4. The attitude of VESPA

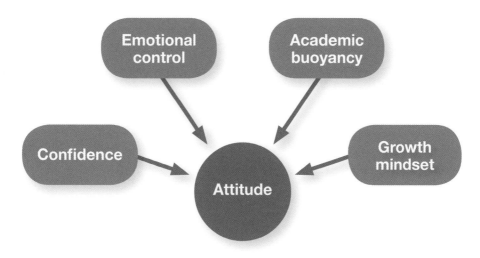

Table 1.1. Summary of attitude

Confidence	Feels confident in attempting new or difficult tasks.
Emotional control	Can regulate their emotions, even in challenging situations.
Academic buoyancy	Responds positively to critical feedback.
Growth mindset	Believes that intelligence can be developed with hard work.

steps; however, the more we celebrate achievements and recognise when pupils are making progress, the more confident they will become. According to Muijs and Reynolds (2011, p. 148), 'The effect of achievement on self-concept is stronger than the effect of self-concept on achievement.'

Emotional control can have a negative effect on pupils, particularly at exam time. No matter how well a pupil has prepared, if they can't control their emotions when they walk into an exam room, there is a chance they won't achieve the grades they deserve.

Academic buoyancy is key to the GCSE years. Pupils have to see critical feedback as a way of improving. Pupils who can't get back up after one disappointing grade can spiral in confidence and emotional control.

Table 1.2. Summarising the links to other constructs

	Vision	Effort	Systems	Practice	Attitude
Grit	✓	✓			
Growth mindset		✓			✓
Resilience					✓
Meta-cognition	✓	✓	✓	✓	✓
Self-efficacy	✓				✓
Conscientiousness		✓	✓	✓	
Self-control	✓	✓			✓

Figure 1.5. The VESPA feedback loop

Finally, we mentioned in the introduction the importance of a growth mindset. A pupil must feel they can improve if they keep working hard. The belief that intelligence is fixed or gifted can limit the other three aspects. Get the attitude right and there is a good chance that a pupil will achieve the best they can be.

This summary of research isn't comprehensive and there are still significant gaps in the evidence base. We are still at the early stages of this journey but we are cautiously optimistic about the promise of future research.

As we discussed in the introduction, a number of constructs are being used within education to explain academic achievement. In Table 1.2, we've attempted to show how the constructs map to the VESPA model.

Closing the Feedback Loop

We feel that the VESPA model questionnaire (discussed in Chapter 14) and tools provide teachers and pupils with a complete feedback loop. In explaining self-regulation strategies, Zimmerman (2001, p. 5), refers to this type of loop as 'a process in which pupils monitor the effectiveness of the learning methods or strategies and respond to this feedback in a variety of ways ranging from covert changes in self-perception to overt changes in behaviour, such as replacing one learning strategy with another'. The model

can be used to conceptualise the idea with teachers and pupils, the tools can be used to develop pupils on the VESPA scales and the questionnaire can be used to identify the areas that need developing and also to measure the impact of any intervention (see Figure 1.5).

From Passive Learners to Active Learners

In summary, the aim of developing pupils on the VESPA scales is to move them from being passive recipients of academic content to active learners who can manage their own learning. The ambition is to have pupils who set and own their own goals, know what effort looks like in their context, manage their own workload using a variety of strategies, understand the importance of deliberate practice and develop a growth mindset.

In contrast, we are finding that some schools are creating environments where their learners are extremely passive in the learning process, particularly where there is a culture of fear among the senior leaders and teachers. Where there is a culture of fear it often leads to the micromanagement of both staff and pupils. In turn, individuals take less responsibility and feel that they have very little control over their outcomes. This usually leads to passivity, where both pupils and staff are waiting for the next set of instructions.

We would argue that this has a damaging effect on both teachers and pupils, and ultimately isn't sustainable. We believe that VESPA and the tools offer a scaffolding solution to part of this problem. VESPA is only one conceptual model; there are many others available. It can be useful to take aspects of various models and make the best fit within your context.

2. Using This Book

Chapters 3–11: The Shape of the Year

When we were putting together *The A Level Mindset*, we decided to have five distinct sections to the book – vision, effort, systems, practice and attitude – under which we organised the tools we'd designed and tested for improving these non-cognitive skills with pupils. All pretty straightforward.

We felt *The GCSE Mindset* called for something different. Having taught GCSE courses for a combined forty years – an alarming thought! – we knew that the shape of Year 11, and the specific challenges and traumas it brings, suggested a chronological rather than thematic organisation of tools. So this is what we've done.

You'll find chapter headings (Chapters 3–11) that refer to months of the academic year rather than non-cognitive skills. For each month, we outline what we feel to be one of the main themes and challenges of that month. It might not fit your experience of GCSE teaching – these things are ultimately subjective – but we hope it aligns roughly.

We used the Change Curve alongside our own experiences of teaching in Year 10 and 11 to decide which challenges should go where. You may well be familiar with this, but if not, the Change Curve is based on a model originally developed in the 1960s by psychologist Elisabeth Kübler-Ross to explain the phases people go through during the grieving process (Figure 2.1). Kübler-Ross proposed that a terminally ill patient would progress through certain stages of grief when informed of their illness. Nowadays, the curve is used to help people understand their reactions to significant changes in their lives.

We've found that starting GCSEs is a significant change in any pupil's life and, like any change, it's likely that they will experience some of the following feelings.

» **Rejection:** 'I don't believe what you're telling me about GCSE study. It doesn't seem any different. I'll carry on as normal.'

» **Denial/minimisation:** 'I'm fine. It'll be alright. Stop hassling me about how different it is.'

» **Anger:** 'I actually hate this. The teachers are rubbish. The subjects are nothing like they said they would be. I wish I could just be in Year 7 again. Remember those days before teachers got all stressy and serious?'

» **Blame self:** 'It turns out I'm just not clever enough to do this.'

» **Anxiety:** 'Everyone else is better than me. I'm missing deadlines. I'm not sleeping well. I don't understand the work. I'm not enjoying this challenge at all. I'm scared I'll fail.'

» **Emotional fog:** Withdrawing effort, giving up.

Figure 2.1. The Change Curve

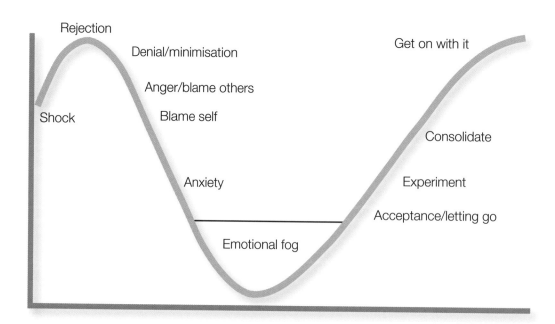

» **Acceptance/letting go:** 'Things are different now. It's hard, but I'm getting to grips with it.'

» **Experiment/consolidate/get on with it:** 'I'm getting better at this. My grades aren't great but they're improving. There are some parts of these courses I like!'

You might want to consider your own school calendar when considering our sequencing. For example, Year 11 mock exams fall in December for us, so that's where a number of practice activities about revision fall. It might be different for you. Are there certain points in the year when you might need to consider where certain activities are placed?

Following the outline of the themes and challenges, you'll find four or five activities that we feel are well suited to that month. Some months you might get vision and effort activities, but nothing on systems or practice. As you approach the exam months, however, you might see a shift to an emphasis on practice, systems and attitude, and less on vision. This isn't an exact science, though, and you might just want to use the activities as you see fit. There's scope, we feel, for running the activities over the course of Year 11 or spacing them out across the two years of Key Stage 4 – but that's up to you.

Using the Activities

Each activity is designed to take fifteen to twenty minutes to complete. Many of them are flexible; they can be delivered to an individual or small group of pupils, a tutor group or a whole cohort.

Think of them as a starting point. As tempting as it might be to import them wholesale into your pastoral curriculum, it's always worth testing and trialling to begin with. Each of us has a different team of colleagues to work with, a different group of senior leaders to whom we are responsible, a different culture which provides a context in which everything else must work, different constraints in terms of time and budget, and different pupils.

It is probably best to start small – try trialling a couple of activities with a single tutor group to see where the sticking points are. Use a handful as part of an intervention group or a one-to-one coaching session. We often work with heads of department who have sufficient accurate data to isolate those pupils who are underperforming but who really struggle with designing intervention sessions that have any effect on progress. We remember being at this stage too – working from a position that assumed underperformance was the result of cognition and designing 'can't do' interventions, such as reteaching the pupils a tricky section of the course, designing an after-school session in which pupils plan and write an exam response together, going over a difficult question again or retesting the pupils. It's often, therefore, a matter of real frustration when we realise that many of the pupils who are below target aren't in our intervention session because they can't do the work. They're cognitively well capable but they've got non-cognitive deficiencies. These activities are designed to encourage reflection on those.

If there are activities which don't strike you as applicable or useful, don't use them! We once asked a tutor team to review all of the VESPA activities we'd been working with over the course of the year. The tutors, sitting in teams, had to pick one activity they always felt comfortable leading and one they hated. The plan, straightforwardly enough, was to axe the ones staff disliked. But we couldn't reach any sort of consensus; activities that some staff steered well clear of were enjoyed by others. It's a personal thing.

Finally, these activities are not recipes. You can tinker, adjust, mess with or completely change what we've given you here. The more you do this, actually, the greater the ownership you and your fellow tutors have over the programme, and the more likely it is to become embedded.

A word on the language of the activity sheets: the tasks themselves are written with a pupil audience in mind, so they take a less formal and looser approach to referencing studies and academic journals, but we give you the details in the introduction to each section.

Chapters 12, 13 and 14: Coaching and Implementation

Chapter 12 is about coaching. We've designed all the tools so they can be used with an individual or group. This chapter explains how you can use VESPA when coaching a pupil.

Chapter 13 takes you through the implementation of VESPA and provides some suggestions on how you might set up a GCSE mindset in your school.

Chapter 14 is by our guest writers, Dr Neil Dagnall and Dr Andrew Denovan from Manchester Metropolitan University. They take you through the research process behind our VESPA questionnaire. In today's educational environment, where empirical data is valued so highly, it's hard to convince people to take these skills seriously if you can't measure them. The questionnaire can be used to measure the impact of interventions but, more importantly, it provides a useful starting point in a conversation with your pupils. Many thanks to Neil and Andrew for supporting our work, helping us to design the questionnaire and contributing to this book.

3. September

Start with the Why

Why do we study history? Why is there a GCSE course in French? Why English literature but not, say, the history of fine art (at the time of writing)? Why media studies? Difficult as these questions are, the final year of Key Stage 4 deserves some discussion of *why*. That's a daunting prospect, so here's a simple approach to take with pupils.

We need educated people to make the world a better place. We're beset with exciting challenges and tricky problems, and we're surrounded by amazing opportunities. We need the next generation of thinkers, problem solvers and creators. Purposeful and exciting work draws on a range of characteristics, skills and knowledge drawn from a broad base. Every course a pupil takes feeds that connected awareness and understanding.

Connect problems with courses and education takes on new colour and meaning. Here's just one example for GCSE geography. Climate change and rising sea levels presents us with a huge challenge. The solutions will come from the next two or three generations of pupils, some of whom will be responsible for specific breakthroughs, while others will change attitudes or drive policy. Spend a short session mapping out the parts of the solution: we need geographers to understand the process and immediate impact, scientists and engineers to study energy expenditure and suggest alternative renewables, designers to create products that are more efficient, entrepreneurs to market, monetise and change public opinion, politicians to make policy, campaign managers to lobby parliament and so on.

Now encourage pupils to consider other challenges and opportunities and connect them with bodies of knowledge and sets of skills being taught every day. Not everything needs to be a desperate, high stakes battle for the future, of course! Culture and entertainment are central to the well-being of a healthy society. Communication and creativity are crucial; technology and innovation are too.

September is the time to address the why, and to create a sense of purpose and meaning. So how can you go about setting some energising and effective goals with pupils? One way is to separate it from talk of careers or IAG (information, advice and guidance).

Goal Setting vs. IAG

Goal setting is entirely distinct from careers IAG, and you should encourage your tutors and pupils to think in these terms too. Many tutors will feel that as teachers we're not best equipped to give clear and effective advice about the jobs market. With the exponential growth of information technologies and the rise of globalisation, we have to accept instead that schools are preparing young people for jobs or careers that either don't currently exist or that teachers know nothing about. Case in point: a recent KPMG report claims that driverless cars will create 320,000 jobs in the UK (KPMG, 2015). How do we translate that into effective classroom IAG?

Goal setting conversations that start, 'What job would you like to do when you're older?' or 'Is there a career you have in mind?' are potentially misguided. But because this approach may have been previously prevalent, the pupils you work with might expect goal setting to be the equivalent of job selection. To be clear: goal setting is best when it is distinct from discussions about various trades and professions. Try to keep 'doctor', 'lawyer', 'plumber', 'astronaut', 'teacher' or 'journalist' out of the vocabulary of goal setting, even if a pupil wants it there. ('You like working outdoors? OK, have you thought about being a gardener?' is the antithesis of what we mean by goal setting or vision building.) We're in no position to predict what current jobs may be automated or just obsolete by the time our pupils enter the employment market. Do your teachers and tutors a favour – lighten their psychological load. Remove them from a place they understandably feel uncomfortable by being explicit – we're not setting long-term job-related goals.

But if we're not discussing the job market, what *are* we going to explore? We think the job of a good tutor is to teach young people the process of goal setting, not to lead the selection of the goal. Derek Sivers, entrepreneur and consultant, has a liberating and refreshing take that captures much of the spirit of good goal setting. If, as we mentioned earlier, goal setting is committing to a vision of the future, Sivers points out: 'what I think is really important is to not commit to one idea of the future that you have'.*

Here, then, is a key element of successful goal setting. Specific goals are by their nature fragile. Visions of the future cannot be so singular that an isolated setback destroys them. American movies may teach us that anyone with a super-specific goal and a ton of persistence can make it, but we all know we need a more nuanced approach. Creating pupils who are persistent in their pursuit of impossibility isn't what we want. The pupil who at 15 wants to study material science at Oxford has a specific and therefore vulnerable goal. By encouraging the idea that it can and will happen if you just keep believing, we entrench an expectation of a single version of the future. If something goes wrong in a chemistry exam at the end of Year 13, the goal is denied, and we run the risk of persistently

chasing it. 'Reapply next year!' we might advise. Or we might reach for, 'Maybe it just wasn't meant to be.'

So what's the alternative? Fatalism? A dour realism that puts the brakes on aspiration? Emphatically no. 'Instead,' Sivers argues, 'commit to a problem that you want to solve. Then you can stay committed to the problem, and continually try to find the ongoing and ever-changing answer to that problem.' If we express a goal as a problem (or another useful idea, a purpose) we create something flexible and resilient to change. If we commit to a problem and purpose we have a reason for a direction of travel. 'Stay committed to the problem and don't attach yourself too much to any given answer that you've come up with at any point,' says Sivers. All of us have worked with pupils who, when writing their personal statements, can't express why they want to do something or have never considered why they want to pursue a particular course. Good goal setting, like so many other things, starts with why.

What Do We Mean By 'Problem and Purpose'?

Imagine two pupils. One commits to a problem and purpose, expressed as a series of questions, like this: 'Is public healthcare in the UK consistently excellent? If not, why not?

* The transcript from Sivers' talk at the World Domination Summit is available at: https://sivers.org/wds.

How can I improve the situation for patients from all walks of life?'

Another commits to a fragile and specific goal: 'I want to study medicine at Leicester University.'

There are weaknesses, like fault lines, built in to the second pupil's goal. One bad exam sees the entire plan destroyed. And the pupil knows this; all year they're jumpy, anxious, stressed. Everything depends on this one result. The joy they might have felt about the goal at some uncluttered, simpler time in the past has gone. The energetic research, reading and thinking that might have once occurred is sacrificed for mechanical repetition of course content and past papers.

Pupil one, meanwhile, knows that there are uncontrollables ahead; exam questions they can't predict, interview curveballs that are impossible to anticipate. It doesn't matter – they know their purpose and the problems that interest them in the world. That's the direction of travel.

In our previous book, *The A Level Mindset*, we share an activity called Twenty Questions. The gist of the activity is that discussing goals works best obliquely, tangentially and personally, rather than directly. So the question, 'What's your life goal?' – blunt, direct and challenging as it is – doesn't

stimulate a rich discussion, but questions like these do:

1 If you could only take one subject, what would it be and why?

2 What lessons or elements of study do you find easy?

3 Describe an interesting lesson you had recently. Why was it interesting?

4 What jobs do you avoid doing, and why?

5 When does time fly? What are you doing?

(Check out Twenty Questions for other discussion points like these.) The two vision activities that follow are designed like this – they are intended to explore themes and threads of vision, not to generate something super-specific.

1. Vision Activity: The Motivation Diamond

Sometimes it's easier to express the motivations and desires that are important to us rather than the jobs or courses that might fulfil them. Professor Steven Reiss, who worked as a psychologist at Ohio State University, conducted studies with over 6,000 people to try to define their underlying motivations. He concluded his work by suggesting there are sixteen different motivations that guide all human behaviour. We've adjusted his list a little to make it more accessible and easy to work with. There are fifteen in ours.

Study the list below and decide which seem as though they might be most important to you. Once you've shortlisted nine of the fifteen, you then have to prioritise them using the diamond. At the top of the diamond, leading the others, should be the motivation that beats all others for you. Underneath, you can have two deputies alongside each other. Then come the rest.

Fifteen possible motivations (adapted from Steven Reiss for the purposes of this task):

1. Acceptance: the need for approval, support and good feeling from those around you.

2. Competition: the need to pit yourself against others – to compete and win.

3. Curiosity: the need to learn, explore, research, discover and try new things.

4. Creativity: the need to design, write, draw, build – to create art or entertainment.

5. Family: the need to raise or help children, to nurture others or to work in small, loyal units supporting those around you.

6. Honour: the need to be loyal to the key values of a group or society – to observe the rules, do what is expected and guide others in these values.

7. Idealism: the need for fairness, equality and social justice.

8. Independence: the need for individuality – the ability to organise and run things your way.

9. Order: the need for organised, stable, predictable environments; creating routines and patterns.

10. Physical activity: the need for movement, exercise and physical challenge.

11. Power: the need for influence, the ability to determine the direction of others; the responsibility for the performance of groups.

12. Saving: the need to collect things, to own things and categorise or order them.

13. Social contact: the need for friends, to have extensive peer relationships.

14. Social status: the need to appear to be of a high social standing or a person of importance.

15. Tranquillity: the need to be calm, relaxed and safe.

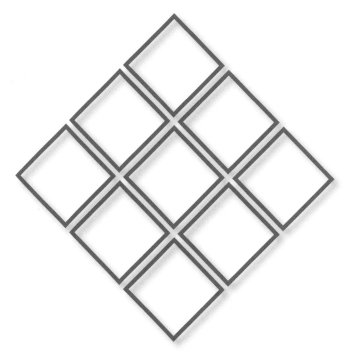

Once you've drawn up your leading motivations, think about the times in your life when you are at your most energised. Times when you're buzzing with excitement, good feeling and happiness.

» What are you doing?

» What elements of your motivation are being rewarded?

» If you had to design a crazy, impossible, perfect job that satisfied these motivations, what would it be?

2. Vision Activity: Problem Not Job, aka The Personal Compass

Entrepreneur Derek Sivers argues that to have a single, specific goal in mind can be limiting – because if obstacles keep cropping up to stop us, we eventually abandon this single, specific goal. Instead of a specific goal, he argues that we should spend our lives *pursuing the answer to a problem*. That's our purpose in life. This is a better way to goal set because even when obstacles block our way, we find another route towards solving our chosen problem – of pursuing our purpose.

For example, here are two pretty similar pupils:

Pupil 1 has a super-specific goal: I want to study medicine at Manchester University and become a doctor.

Pupil 2 has a problem that fascinates them: how can we improve healthcare in the UK?

Of course, each pupil will encounter obstacles along their way. But if pupil 1 doesn't get the grades to study medicine at Manchester, the route to their goal is blocked. If the same thing happens to pupil 2, they will find a different route to solving the problem that fascinates them; they may do voluntary work, start a nursing course, choose a degree that covers public healthcare systems or research the politics of healthcare.

Sivers says that if we can express our goals *as problems we're trying to solve*, we always know when we're heading in the right direction and we tend not to be put off by obstacles. Let's build a compass. Your true north is the problem that most fascinates you – the one you should always be heading towards. Let's call this your *lead problem*. Around true north (north-east, north-west) are other problems that are close to your lead problem – perhaps different versions of your lead problem. If you're heading in this direction you're still doing OK. Around the other compass points (east, south and west) are distractions – things you shouldn't be pursuing, *even if other people think you should*. If you're going in these directions, you'll need to turn back.

Cover the compass points with notes. Problems that interest or fascinate you go at or near your true north. Distractions go elsewhere, with the biggest at the south – the opposite direction to your true north.

Example problems to consider, discuss or discard include:

» How do we make the distribution of wealth in the UK fairer?

» How can we save larger numbers of species from extinction?

» How might we design buildings that increase people's happiness and well-being?

» What are the elements necessary for a superb movie?

» How can we improve pupils' experience of school, college or university?

» How can the design of _____ be improved?

» How can we accelerate our progress towards curing _____?

» How can art be used to improve people's lives?

» What qualities are necessary for huge success in _____?

» How can I create popular, immersive, interactive computer games?

» How can we reduce crime by working with young offenders?

» What qualities make some _____ better than others?

» How can we help people cope with difficult, stressful or traumatic times in their lives?

» What does outstanding parenting/teaching look like?

» How can we discover more about the workings of the universe?

» How do we solve global warming?

» What does augmented/virtual reality mean for media/entertainment/gaming?

» How can we work more efficiently using artificial intelligence?

Once you think you have some interesting problems you'd like to explore further, use a piece of paper to sketch out some next steps. Is there a documentary you could watch, a book you can read, someone you could talk to or ask for advice, or a piece of research you can do to get more information?

3. Effort Activity: Mission and Medal

Effort is just a habit. Pupils who have the effort habit have created a weekly routine of repeated activities that allow them to respond to teacher requests (homework) and reinforce learning (independent work). Pupils without the effort habit have little or no routine and respond to work as and when it hits them.

Increasing your levels of effort can be a tiring task because it means moving away from a comfortable and familiar way of working into a less comfortable one. So rewarding yourself for increased levels of effort is hugely important. Parents and teachers might not spot the change in your work patterns right away, so it will be up to you to give yourself a pat on the back.

That's where mission and medal comes in: *the mission is the work, the medal is the reward!* This activity helps you to design and structure an effortful week of work that you can then repeat until it becomes a routine. Pretty soon you won't be the only person rewarding yourself – teachers, tutors and parents will spot your new routine and you'll be in line for some praise!

Step 1: Audit of a Typical Week

Before you design your mission and medal week, you need to figure out what's currently happening. In the space below, record what you do with your time during a typical week. It might be the week just gone or the week you're in. Make a note of what work you do, where you do it and how much productive work gets done in each section of the day.

Are there particular slots that work best for you? Are there slots that are hopeless – times when you find it very difficult to work or where you sit down to work but you don't get anything done?

	Before school (early morning – 7am–8.30am)	During school (morning and early afternoon – 9am–3pm)	After school (twilight – 4pm–5.30pm)	Evening (7pm–9.30pm)
Monday				
Tuesday				
Wednesday				
Thursday				
Friday				
Saturday				
Sunday				

Step 2: Creating a Mission and Medal Week

For five of the seven days, set yourself a *sixty minute mission*. It might be to complete homework, plan ahead, consolidate learning, organise notes, research sixth form colleges, fill out an application or begin a revision guide. Complete the mission all at once or in parts. Choose times of day when you work well – without distractions.

For the same five days, set aside *a medal to be awarded on completion of the mission*. It might be a session on your games console, a TV programme, a football match, some time on social media, something nice to eat or drink or some favourite music. Vary your medals.

Don't forget to assign yourself two *bonus* medals – a mid-weeker to pep you up and a Sunday-nighter to get you feeling good for the week. These medals should be a little larger than your regular medals.

	Before school (early morning – 7am–8.30am)	During school (morning and early afternoon – 9am–3pm)	After school (twilight – 4pm–5.30pm)	Evening (7pm–9.30pm)
Monday				
Mission:				
Medal:				
Tuesday				
Mission:				
Medal:				
Wednesday				
Mission:				
BONUS medal:				
Thursday				
Mission:				
Medal:				
Friday				
Saturday				
Sunday				
Mission:				
BONUS medal:				

In this example, you've been given Friday evening and all day Saturday off. You might want to adjust these depending on what you do with your time – feel free to! Choose exciting medals which make you feel good about the work you've done!

Building a Scoreboard

There's a lot of conflicting research about how long it takes to create a habit. Unless you keep track you'll have no idea. Now you've devised a mission and medal week, you can use a scoreboard as a simple way of helping you with motivation.

We developed this idea after hearing the American comedian Jerry Seinfeld talk about how he writes jokes. He sets himself the goal of writing a joke every day and keeps a diary to check off when he's been successful. His argument is that once you see the days being ticked off, you don't want to see the pattern being broken, so you keep going. After a few weeks, this new behaviour just becomes a habit and you might not even need to think about it – you just do it!

So, for every day you follow your mission and medal programme, you simply tick off the days. You'll need a monthly calendar like the one below.

Sunday	Monday	Tuesday	Wednesday	Thursday	Friday	Saturday
		~~1~~	~~2~~	~~3~~	~~4~~	~~5~~
~~6~~	~~7~~	~~8~~	~~9~~	~~10~~	11	12
13	14	15	16	17	18	19
20	21	22	23	24	25	26
27	28	29	30	31		

4. Attitude Activity: Growth Mindset

Carol Dweck is one of the world's leading researchers in the field of motivation and is a professor of psychology at Stanford University. She's developed a theory about our attitude towards learning. She says that people generally fall into two categories: a fixed mindset or a growth mindset. Some of the characteristics are shown in the table below.

Fixed mindset	Growth mindset
Feels threatened by the success of others.	Finds lessons and inspiration in the success of others.
Ignores useful feedback.	Learns from criticism.
Sees effort as fruitless or worthless.	Sees effort as the path to mastery.
Gives up easily.	Persists in the face of setbacks.
Avoids challenge.	Embraces challenge.
Desires to look smart.	Desires to learn.

Dweck has developed a questionnaire that helps you to think about your mindset. This can be done here on her mindset website: http://mindsetonline.com/testyourmindset/step1.php.

To give you a quick indication of your mindset try the questionnaire below:

	Item	Mostly agree	Mostly disagree
1	Your intelligence is something very basic that you can't change very much.		
2	You can learn new things but you can't really change how intelligent you are.		
3	No matter how much intelligence you have, you can always change it quite a bit.		
4	You can always substantially change how intelligent you are.		

Scoring and Interpretation

Items 1 and 2 are fixed mindset questions and items 3 and 4 are growth mindset questions. Which mindset did you agree with more? You will be a mixture, but most people lean one way or the other about certain things and at certain times.

What did you learn about yourself? Where do you have fixed mindset thinking and where do you have more of a growth mindset? What could you do to change?

The Language of Mindsets

Finally, we often find that pupils express their attitudes towards learning through the things they say. We've listed fifteen phrases we've heard pupils tell us before now. Sort them into fixed and growth mindset statements. Is there a particular statement you can use to reassure yourself and encourage greater positivity about learning?

1. I've never been good at maths.

2. I just need to get some more practice in.

3. I'm hopeless at this.

4. Maybe if I was cleverer this would be achievable.

5. This doesn't come naturally to me.

6. A couple of hours of intense study and I reckon I can crack this problem.

7. I've just not got a brain for English/maths/science.

8. I'm going to take a break and come back refreshed. I'll make some progress then.

9. I'm not a creative person.

10. Let me have another go at this – I'll get better.

11. I must have missed something. I just need to go back and check I've got this clear in my head.

12. I've not totally understood this yet. I'm going to go over it again.

13. I can't do this. I'll never be able to do this.

14. This topic is impossible. I'm just going to hope it doesn't come up in the exam.

15. _____ is lucky. They're just naturally brilliant at it. I'm not.

Finally, if you'd like to learn more about growth mindsets, there are some fun videos here: https://ideas.classdojo.com/b/growth-mindset.

4. October

Mapping the Journey

It's worth remembering that you might have ridden the Year 11 rollercoaster five, ten or twenty times, but for the pupils in front of you, it's their first and last go. The cheerful ease with which you navigate the year is impossible for them. You know every dip, curve and loop of this ride back to front, but they're staring at a tangle of unreadable tracks through a fogbank. OK, metaphor over: the point is that we've sometimes found ourselves assuming that pupils know the terrain ahead and forgetting that it's entirely new for them.

Your first thought, like ours, might be to provide everyone with a handy calendar. There's your map, folks; it tells you what's going to happen in October, November, December and so on. A calendar is important, sure. But it occurred to us more recently, what about maps that can help pupils to navigate the psychological terrain ahead? Your learners will benefit from knowing the emotional shape of their journey so they can prepare for it and even anticipate some of the trials and tribulations that await them.

Here's something to make clear to your pupils: the trials and tests ahead will come from three sources: the unexpected and external and internal influences. Using a diagram like this is a good way to illustrate what's going to hit them as the year unfolds and the exams approach.

Figure 4.1. Trials and tests ahead

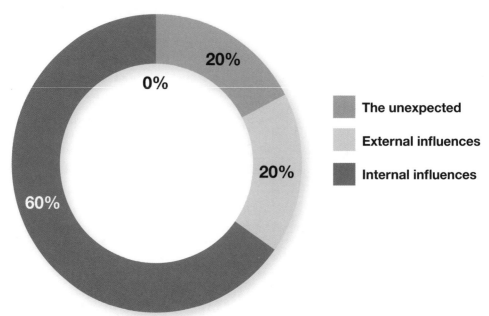

The percentages here are not based on research – they're illustrative, and you can adjust them any way you feel comfortable. But working with thousands of pupils over the last twenty years, we've come to see internal influences to be the biggest of the three issues. Keep this percentage in the majority; the largest proportion of problems the pupils face will come from themselves.

Ask them to make a list of things that might come under the three headings. You can give them a few ideas to get started:

» **Unexpected.** An argument with their parents, an older sibling moving back into their bedroom after a university place doesn't work out, a teacher leaving and being replaced, a relationship ending, a fight

on the street, a grandparent being taken ill. These things – always out of our control – come along to make life more complicated. Events like this continue to confound and challenge us, so your messages need to focus on the inevitability of these changes and challenges. We can't duck out. We need to be ready for them; they happen to everybody and, eventually, everybody finds a way to cope and adjust.

» **External.** Homework, tasks in lessons, tests and preparation, mock exams, college applications, coursework submissions, multiple deadlines making for super-busy weeks. These issues can be anticipated. Make this clear any way you want: some of these challenges might be better flagged and communicated than others, some might arrive more obviously than others, but we're always going to expect them. In this way, it's not going to be like some huge injustice when they happen.

» **Internal.** Lack of vision, loss of energy and effort, perfectionism, disorganisation, procrastination, fear, complacency. Pupils will have a field day exploring their fallibilities here.

The message you want to emerge should be around the source of the challenges. Pupils are often floored by problems because they're looking in the wrong direction. Understandably, they're expecting external or unexpected challenges, but they're not ready for the realisation (it's happened to all of us at some point or another) that *they are the problem*. Here's where the idea of psychological self-sabotage can be explored. Ask pupils to discuss or attempt a definition of the phrase. Stay away from physical sabotage (self-harm, problem eating) and put your focus on faulty or misfiring habits, attitudes or approaches to study which reduce our capacity to do good work.

Once this work is done, you can begin exploring the idea that, leaving aside the unexpected which can strike at any time, certain internal challenges might arrive at

predictable points in the year. We're all different, of course, and this needs constant emphasis, but there might also be broad similarities between the psychological journeys we take – and this can be a reassuring realisation.

Mapping Trouble 1: Three Key Months

The emotional response to trauma has been mapped by the American psychologist Elisabeth Kübler-Ross, and her Change Curve is one of the maps we use in *The A Level Mindset*. For the purposes of this book, we've used Paul Graham's emotional and psychological map, referred to here in its adapted form as 'The Process'; it was originally called 'The Startup Curve' and was designed to document the challenges of building a company from scratch.* This adjusted version, a sort of line graph by time, shows the peaks and troughs that anyone might experience when beginning a major new challenge.

Figure 4.2 is a light-hearted, comic look at our response to challenge. Share it with pupils! For us, October half-term marks the 'wearing off of novelty', mock exam preparation in November is the 'trough of sorrow', that dip beneath the line in the centre is January and those 'wiggles of false hope' come sometime

* The Startup Curve was originally designed by Paul Graham of Y Combinator and appears on the *Business Insider* website: http://www.businessinsider.com/chart-of-the-day-the-startup-curve-2012-3?IR=T.

Figure 4.2. The Process

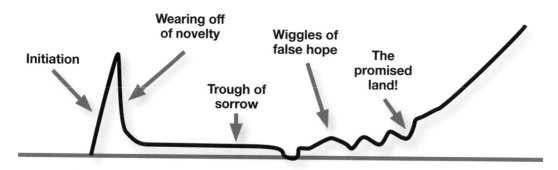

in the spring. By giving pupils a glimpse into what December, January and February might hold, you're illustrating the potential challenges ahead and emphasising the fact that we can all figure out a way through them, just like last year's Year 11s and the year before them. (We're fond of Seth Godin's observation about growth and progress: in his book, *Poke the Box*, he says, 'The path is well-lit.') Older siblings, cousins, friends of friends and sixth-formers can all tell them a little more about the journey.

You might want to ask pupils to label some of the internal challenges that might manifest at different stages of the year. Tell them everyone will ride a line something like Graham's, but we all go at different speeds, and everyone – without exception – will reach the end. Tell them that they can use the energy of the good times to drive them through more challenging periods. These journeys are personal, so you might (or might not, depending on your group) want to label what

we often consider to be the three key months of the final year of an academic course: September ('initiation' – a burst of energy), January (that gloomy little dip in Graham's 'trough of sorrow') and March (early signs of 'the promised land'). Explain that if they handle themselves well at these key inflection points along the way, they will put themselves in a very good position to perform to their potential. We've enjoyed admitting that 'The Process' also represents the psychological journey taken by the class teacher each year, too – from the delight of meeting a new class in early September, through the hopeless feelings accompanying a slew of poor test results in January, to the growing sense of possibility as spring comes. The point is that by normalising these psychological and emotional experiences, we go some way to ensuring that pupils feel normal when they experience difficult times.

Mapping Trouble 2: Drawing the Journey

It's interesting to see similar approaches used elsewhere. A pupil at Manchester Metropolitan University shared a different mapping activity with us. Her course was all about maps in a way; she was a landscape architect. One of the activities her tutors encouraged her to do at the beginning of her post-graduate qualification was to draw a map representing the personal challenges she would face during the year. Pupils were given ideas and examples before being sent away to complete their map.

Here's an extract from the map she produced:

It's a powerful reminder of the challenges (represented here as geographical obstacles), but also the support that exists when pupils begin learning journeys. The map includes networks of support as well as tricky currents and sharp rocks. Crucially, beyond the dotted line that leaves the picture in the top right-hand corner, it reaches a successful conclusion ('Success!' the pupil writes – 'Dry Land') – something that needs constant re-emphasis during activities like these.

Have a look at both The Roadmap (Activity 5) and Network Audits (Activity 12) for pupil tasks that might feed into a trouble-mapping exercise like this.

Credit: Jo Phillips (used with permission).

5. Vision Activity: The Roadmap

Sometimes setting a goal can feel like a long process. The goals can seem so distant that we don't take any immediate action. Designing a success map can really help with this. A success map is a visual reminder of the journey you're going on. It guides you to where you want to be and warns you about things that might pull you off course.

Here's what you need to do. First, you need to go to the end of the map and write down the goal you want to achieve. In the same box it's useful to include the date by which you want to achieve your goal.

Underneath the goal box you'll see 'why'. Here you write why achieving the goal is important to you.

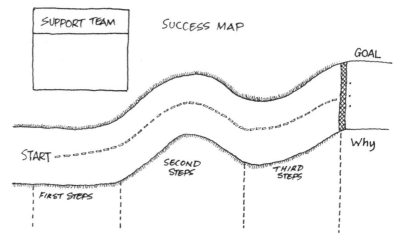

Next, you need to break down the goal into a series of steps in a journey. You might think about these steps as a series of days, weeks or even months. Represent them as a road or pathway – some sort of track that takes you through the difficulties towards a conclusion.

Look at how this university student has used a dotted line to indicate the journey of her boat between the islands in this version of her map on page 57:

There are two main elements here – the positive and the negative. Have a look at how the student emphasises positive things that are going to help: 'Peaceful Bay', 'Exercise', 'Up Early!', 'Mind Maps' and 'Tutors to the Rescue!' And hazards to watch out for: 'Loss of Focus', 'Sharks of Disillusionment' and 'Sea Monsters of Personal Disaster!'.

You can do the same on your map:

» **Mapping your support.** Surround your pathway with good things that will encourage and help you. Rewards, celebrations and holidays all need marking on the map. Think about the people who might support you too. Could you ask friends, a mentor or your parents/guardian? Write the names of these people in your 'support team' box.

» **Mapping your challenges.** Here you should include the things you're going to need to watch out for. They should be specific to you – your bad habits! It might be laziness, procrastination, worry or distraction.

Unlike the example above, we've found it useful to add dates to the map so you know what happens when in the year ahead.

Once done, it's a good idea to keep your map on display somewhere that you can always see it. This will help to remind you of the steps that need to be completed to reach that destination in the distance!

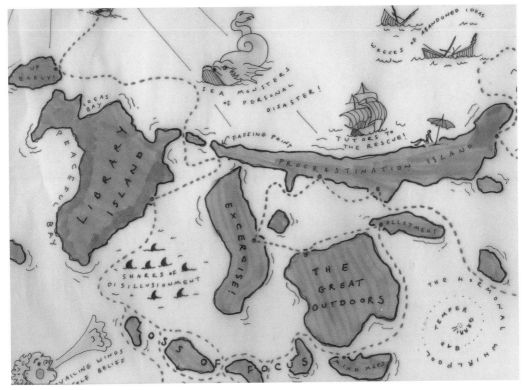

Credit: Jo Phillips (used with permission).

6. Systems Activity: The Weekly Planner

Most pupils have used a calendar for planning their revision at some point. But even at the start of a year, it's worth taking stock of your week. What does a typical week look like for you? Where are the gaps (if there are any) or are you over-committed?

We recently did this with a pupil who was starting to feel very stressed. When he filled in the weekly planner it became very clear why – he literally didn't have a spare minute! To find additional time to get on top of his schoolwork, the only option would have been for him to sleep less (not something we would recommend!). It was apparent that he was committed to too many activities: he was attending swimming sessions three times a week, including all day on Saturday, he helped out at a kids activity session on a Tuesday evening and he was working for his uncle in his shop for eight hours during the week. He was clearly going to burn out before he got to Christmas!

Current vs. Preferred

The first step of this exercise is to record your weekly activities. You can get creative here and use different colours for different activities. Make a note of everything you're doing with your time – school, of course, but also commitments to classes, sport, jobs, helping out at home and so on.

	Before school (early morning – 7am–8.30am)	During school (morning and early afternoon – 9am–3pm)	After school (twilight – 4pm–5.30pm)	Evening (7pm–9.30pm)
Monday				
Tuesday				
Wednesday				
Thursday				
Friday				
Saturday				
Sunday				

The next step is to decide: are you happy with your week? Are there things you'd like to change?

If there are things you would like to change, you need to plan out your preferred week, then complete the table below. This will help you to think through the advantages and disadvantages of making the changes. If the positives outweigh the negatives, you know what needs to be done!

Advantages of making changes	Disadvantages of making changes
Disadvantages of not making changes	**Advantages of not making changes**

7. Vision Activity: The Rule of Three

We borrowed this activity from Jack Canfield's book *The Success Principles* (2005). He is also the author of the 'Chicken Soup for the Soul' series (we would recommend *Chicken Soup for the Teenage Soul* – it's full of supportive stories, reassuring advice and cracking ideas).

Canfield employs the useful analogy of chopping down a tree when trying to achieve your goals. He says that if you take a very sharp axe and take five swings at a tree every day, no matter how big the tree, eventually it will come down. It's the same with any goal you set. If you take a few small steps every month towards achieving your goal, eventually you'll get there, no matter how big the goal.

Canfield almost makes it sound inevitable. It makes you think: the reason people don't achieve their dreams isn't that they lack a dream, it's that they just don't take any action. *A dream is just a dream unless you take action!*

This activity might seem simple, but we guarantee it's one of the most effective tools we have ever used.

All you have to do is take three steps every half-term towards achieving your long-term goal. It's that simple. You have to decide the steps you are going to take and then commit to doing them.

First, remind yourself of your long-term goal:

My goal is: _____.

Then list all the actions that are going to take you closer to achieving that goal. Remember, it's only three small steps per half-term – that's roughly one every two weeks.

	Action steps	Completed
Sept–Oct		
Nov–Dec		
Jan–Feb		
Mar–April		
April–May		
June–July		

When you've completed the table, it's important that you keep it somewhere you can see it. Stick it up in your room or study area. You might find it useful to share it with a friend or parent and ask them to check up on your progress.

8. Systems Activity: Chunking Steps

The higher you progress up the school, the more likely it is that you are going to get pieces of work that require more than one sitting to complete. This means that you will be unlikely to sit down and finish the whole activity or project in one go. Gone are the Key Stage 3 days when most homework could be completed within fifteen or twenty minutes!

Sooner or later you're going to get a piece of homework or coursework that you know is going to take a few hours to complete. At first this can be quite daunting. Often, when we are faced with a large piece of work like this we procrastinate (put it off) because we're not sure where to start.

There's an old Chinese proverb that says, 'A journey of a thousand miles begins with a single step.' Chunking will help you to take that first step.

Here's how it works. Let's imagine that you've decided to run a marathon in a year's time. There are a number of things you might need to do (run a lot of miles is the obvious one!), but you can't go straight out and run twenty-six miles. You first need to break down all the tasks you might need to do:

» Buy some trainers

» Join a running club

» Find a coach

» Run a 10K

» Enter a race

This would be the start of the list – there's much more than we've listed here. The second step is to set yourself some milestones (what you need to have done and by when).

You can use the same process with a long and challenging piece of work. Here are the steps you might need to take:

» **Step 1:** Identify the goal. How will you know when the task is complete? What will it look like? When will it be?

» **Step 2:** Write down everything you will need to do to complete the task – everything you can think of from the start to the end. Your ideas might come out in a crazy order – that's fine! You can sort them out later.

» **Step 3:** Decide the order of activities using the diagram below, adding them to the steps. Don't forget to include a deadline for each step.

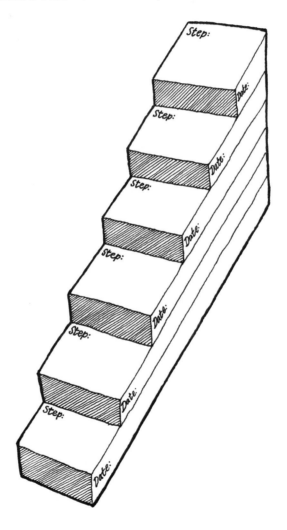

Now pin this up somewhere clear and prominent, and check it regularly!

9. Vision Activity: Grit

We often hear about the term 'grit', but what does it mean and can you measure it?

Grit is about having passion and perseverance for a long-term goal. It's an idea that has been developed by Angela Duckworth, a professor at the University of Pennsylvania. She's spent years looking at grit and how it can be developed. Most people have at least one area where they might have shown grit. For example, you might have started dance classes when you were young and still be dancing ten years later, you might have persisted in developing your skills as a footballer, have been drawing and painting in your spare time for years or have learned to play a musical instrument.

One of the best-known examples of grit is the author J. K. Rowling. Joanne Rowling first got the idea for the Harry Potter series on a delayed train from Manchester to King's Cross station in London. At the time, Rowling was a single parent and living on state benefits. She often did her writing in cafes in Edinburgh, with her young daughter next to her in a pram, because her apartment was so cold and she couldn't afford the heating. She worked on the first Harry Potter book for five years! It was rejected by at least a dozen publishers before being accepted by Bloomsbury. The Harry Potter series has now sold over 450 million copies worldwide. J. K. Rowling's Harvard commencement speech describes the perseverance to continue her love of writing while experiencing professional rejection and doubt. You can watch it here: https://www.youtube.com/watch?v=wHGqp8lz36c.

It's worth remembering that there's no such thing as an overnight success. Most successful people have usually spent years working behind the scenes to develop their craft. They've often shown passion and perseverance for many years before anyone recognised their work. This is true grit.

So, How Gritty Are You?

Below is a version of the Grit Scale developed by Angela Duckworth (Duckworth, 2016, p. 55). Don't think about the questions too much. Just go for your gut feeling and answer the questions in relation to most people.

	Not at all like me = 1	Not much like me = 2	Somewhat like me = 3	Mostly like me = 4	Very much like me = 5
1. New ideas and projects distract me from previous ones.					
2. Setbacks don't discourage me. I don't give up easily.					
3. I often set a goal but later pursue a different one.					
4. I am a hard worker.					
5. I have difficulty maintaining my focus on projects that take more than a few months to complete.					
6. I finish whatever I begin.					
7. My interests change from year to year.					
8. I am diligent. I never give up.					
9. I have been obsessed with an idea or project for a short time but later lost interest.					
10. I have overcome setbacks to conquer an important challenge.					

To calculate your grit score, add up all the points for the boxes and divide by 10. The highest score you can get is 5 (very gritty) and the lowest score is 1 (not at all gritty).

You could discuss your findings with your parents, tutor or friends. Do you think the score is accurate?

When you've discussed the questionnaire answer the questions below:

1. When have I been most gritty?

2. How could I become grittier with my schoolwork?

Remember, you are only young so your grit score hasn't fully developed yet. You might also find it useful to watch Duckworth's famous TED Talk on grit: https://www.ted.com/talks/angela_lee_duckworth_grit_the_power_of_passion_and_perseverance.

5. November

Leading and Lagging Indicators

You may be familiar with the terms leading and lagging indicators. If you aren't, here's a brief introduction. A lagging indicator is something that gives you information or measurement after the fact. It's a product of output. A leading indicator gives you a reading or measurement before the output data arrives, predicting future events. Lagging indicators arrive less frequently but are often clear and reliable readings (*often* is the key word here!). Leading indicators can be observed much more regularly but might be more difficult to quantify.

Having got the definitions out of the way, let's use an example for clarification. Set your pupils this challenge, and they'll get a good sense of what leading and lagging indicators are too. Put them in groups and ask them to investigate the following. Imagine you're trying to lose weight, you tell them, but you're only allowed to use one device to help you. You have two choices: a set of super-accurate weighing scales that stay in your bedroom at home or a highly calibrated pedometer that you carry with you all the time.

One device will operate as a lagging indicator here – the weighing scales. They'll give you output data, a helpfully accurate assessment of your weight. But although they can tell you what happened after the fact, they can't tell you what's happening right now. The other device – the pedometer – offers leading indicator data. It doesn't weigh you but it measures a bunch of factors we know contribute to weight loss, gives continuous feedback and works as a predictor of the future.

Soon enough, the pupils will begin discussing these contrasting features and make their decision. Now throw a spanner in the works:

» If you choose the weighing scales, you can look at them once every twenty days.

» If you choose the pedometer, you can look at it twenty times every day.

Does this alter pupil choices? Here you're clarifying a key feature of leading and lagging indicators – the availability of data versus its accuracy. By choosing the leading indicator you're sacrificing accuracy for timeliness. The lagging indicator sacrifices timeliness for accuracy. More discussion can go on as you explore these issues.

It won't be long before someone wants to know what the hell this has got to do with education. Good question.

Lagging Indicators in the Classroom

Marked work, you can tell your pupils, is a lagging indicator. Depending on the assessment and feedback policies of the school you work in, pupils are getting it once every twenty days or so, just like the weighing scales. Maybe the gap between assessed pieces might be more like thirty days in your organisation, maybe gaps are slightly shorter.

Either way, the final year of Key Stage 4 lasts something like thirty-three weeks. That's maybe eleven or twelve cycles of marking and feedback. Eleven chances to take feedback (or 'check your weight' if we are to pursue this metaphor) and perhaps ten clear opportunities to adjust behaviour and performance. And that's assuming the marked pieces are all checking performance against exam criteria. They might not be. It could be that pupils get fewer than ten chances to change.

Here's another complication. So far, we've assumed lagging indicators are quality data, and that by focusing on them we might not get a timely measurement of pupil performance but at least we get an accurate one, right? Well, depending on the course, this might be open to question. One factor in play is accuracy of assessment. Pupils may come out significantly above or below target because of the way we've designed and marked assessments. Harris Cooper and

Thomas Good (1983, p. 17) write compellingly about 'performance expectations' – that is, the tendency for teachers' assessments to reflect where they perceive the pupil to be rather than provide an accurate measure of exactly how they have performed.

In short: our lagging indicators might not be as accurate as we might hope or suppose. It might be tempting to increase the number of assessed pieces ad infinitum in order to tackle this problem. More regular assessment gives more access to lagging indicator data, more feedback loops and iterations for pupils to improve, and we get to iron out potential outliers caused by inaccurate marking or poorly designed assessments. But do we sacrifice quality of feedback – so central to pupil improvement – by doing so?

Perhaps there is another way of considering the problem.

Leading Indicators in the Classroom

So, what are the 'pedometer activities' on your course? What habits, routines and behaviours are closely linked to success – so close they almost predict it? If you can impress upon your pupils the importance of executing a series of these activities on a daily or weekly basis, you can lock in improved performance in the future without having to return to the scales every week.

But leading indicators are less reliable, you might say. They're fuzzy. The link between the behaviour and the outcome might not be rock solid. Perhaps. But if the lagging indicator we've got – assessed work – isn't providing us with continuous, timely and accurate data either, then perhaps a focus on leading indicators will give us some extra leverage.

Let's take an example. Suppose you spend an hour with a focus group of top performers – pupils who steepened their learning trajectories and performed really well. Cognition won't have played as big a part as we might suppose; underpinning this success will be a series of strategies, tools, habits and routines.

Draw them out and you might find successful pupils have recorded what they want to achieve in each course (vision) or they review their notes after each lesson, recasting them in some way (practice), put in a regular number of proactive study hours each week (effort), find spaces in which they can do deep work and reach some version of a flow state (practice again), sequence and schedule work in a certain way (systems) or maintain a resilient positivity through tough times by relying on a network of friends (attitude).

If a particular technique – for example, 'creating and sticking to a revision timetable that begins at February half-term' (systems)

– is closely aligned with strong exam performance, we have a leading indicator, a pedometer activity. And we can shift our focus to ensuring all pupils execute it. It becomes a course requirement, chased up and challenged with the energy we might usually reserve for missing homework. Other routines might be in evidence right from the start of a course. Let's suppose your focus group discussions surface the fact that successful pupils 'keep lists of difficulties and visit relevant members of staff to clarify understanding' (practice). If this is the case, it could become a regularly checked course requirement.

Once you have a list of leading indicators, you might look for those that transcend course boundaries and support learning despite the specifics of the particular discipline. Advertise these to parents and pupils at the start of the year so expectations are high and clear. Check execution of these behaviours and prepare intervention for those not engaging. The message is clear: these habits and routines are *so closely associated with exam success* that those who do not engage jeopardise future performance.

10. Practice Activity: Building Independent Learning

For some pupils the only work they ever do has been set by their teacher: do you ever do more?

We've found that the top performing pupils are usually setting their own work if their teacher hasn't set it for them. This can be hard, though, particularly if you aren't sure exactly what work to set yourself. Teachers quite often say to pupils that they should be doing 'independent learning' or 'reading around the subject'. But what does that actually mean?

We would suggest that you get much more specific and design your independent learning so that you know exactly what you should be doing and how long it should take you. (Some teachers provide their pupils with this sort of activity, so it might be an activity you can skip. If not, read on.)

Five Independent Learning Activities

For each of your GCSE subjects we suggest that you design five activities.

First, identify the topic. What is it you'd like to spend some more time on?

Second, what are you going to do? Watch a YouTube video, read a book or do some online research? Use the table of suggestions overleaf to get you started, and choose five.

Comparing your work with that of pupils who get higher grades.
Making a clear, visual overview of a course, connecting all the content in a huge diagram/ mind-map.
Creating flashcards as a memory aid.
Reading lots of exam questions and seeing if you can recognise 'types' or 'genres' of question.
Asking for extra work to be assessed and carefully reading the feedback you get.
Creating a glossary of key words with definitions.
Expanding class notes with reference to textbooks.
Representing complicated information visually using a table, chart or diagram.
Reading through an examiners' report and making a list of dos and don'ts.
Choosing a specific area of difficulty and discussing it in detail with a friend.
Planning responses to past exam questions.
Borrowing someone else's class notes and using them to expand yours.
Finding a brilliant course textbook and reading a chapter, making notes as you go.
Watching online videos and interacting with associated VLE resources.
Arranging a meeting with an older student or sibling who has done the course before.
Writing for twenty minutes under timed conditions.

Third, where do you need to go to get access to the resources?

Finally, what activity are you going to do? Remember, doing some active work is going to be more beneficial than passive activities.

Now you've got a plan, complete the table below for each subject. The example below is for GCSE sociology.

Subject: Sociology

Topic	What	Where	Activity
1. Research methods	Watch the first YouTube video on statistics	https://www. youtube.com/ watch?v=PDj S20kic54	Make a mind-map while watching
2.			
3.			
4.			
5.			

11. Systems Activity: Three Types of Attention

Everyone's day moves through phases, and you're probably no different – there are times when you're fired up and raring to go, there are times when your energy levels are just average and there are times when you feel your attention is low and your motivation dips.

These three phases happen to everyone during a working day. You're not unusual if you have low energy levels or can't concentrate; if you catch yourself looking around you and seeing others hard at work, remember they're no different to you – they're just in a different phase of their day.

Some people can predict when they're going to be feeling fired up (it might be the mornings, it might be after breakfast or after exercise) and when they're going to feel slower. Others haven't noticed a pattern, but once they pay attention they see one emerging. For others, it's totally random.

Graham Allcott, founder of Think Productive (http://thinkproductive.co.uk), uses the following definitions for the three states:

1. Proactive attention (fully focused, fired up, feeling fresh).

2. Active attention (plugged in, ticking along nicely).

3. Inactive attention (flagging, fried, foggy).

He argues that really successful people get work done in all three states. They don't give up when they're in state 3, they just switch tasks.

Make a list of all the tasks you've got on your plate at the moment. Think of everything – homework, reading, essays, revision, upcoming tests, college interviews, etc.

Now categorise them. Complex and challenging tasks go in 'proactive attention'. When you feel fully focused, fired up and fresh, you tackle those. Regular tasks go in 'active attention'. They're tasks to get on with when you feel you're ticking along nicely. Repetitive tasks that are pretty easy go in 'inactive attention'. When you're feeling fried or foggy, you switch to those tasks.

Proactive attention	Active attention	Inactive attention

Keep the list with you for a week or two. Whenever you're about to start working:

» Check your energy levels. Sit still for a second and listen to your body. Decide which attention state you're in.

» Review the list of tasks you've got to do that suit your attention level. If there are none in that column, find one from the next column and tackle it.

After a week or two, see whether you can observe patterns in your attention levels. Really good learners have noticed these patterns in themselves and sequence their tasks beforehand.

12. Attitude Activity: Network Audits

Sometimes it's easy to forget how many people want to help you succeed. Each of us has a significant network of support around us, but it's a natural tendency sometimes to think, 'If I ask for help it must mean I'm failing. I need to do this alone.'

But seeking help just makes everything easier. So don't believe the story that goes, 'One day I'll have to stand on my own two feet. I may as well start now.' As you grow up and face new challenges, there will *always* be people around you who can help; someone who's done it before and can give you some advice. Nowadays, that help is just a search engine away – you can contact experts in thousands of fields through social media. You could spend a very successful life continually asking for help!

But still the myth persists that we must do it alone. This activity should support you in auditing (that means listing and organising) every single person who could be on your team. And from there, you can decide who you need to help you with some upcoming challenges.

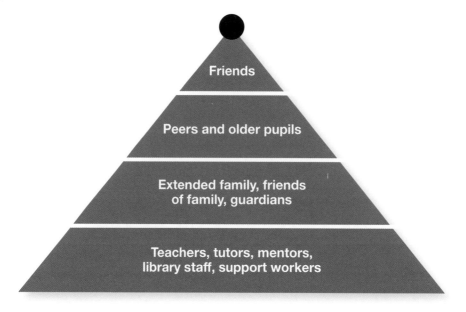

You're the dot at the top and underneath you is a team of people all waiting for the chance to support you. First, make a list of everyone you can think of that fits into the categories above.

» Think of friends you have at school, but also those you might have outside of school, on social media or at other schools.

» Who among your peers has the potential to help you out? Who, a few years older, has gone through this already? Who's an expert on the subjects you're struggling with? Which of your friends has an older brother or sister you could speak to?

» Think about your parents, of course, but also aunties, uncles, cousins and family friends.

» You attend a school where every paid member of staff has a genuine interest in helping you improve. Your first thoughts might be your own teachers, but what about other staff members – librarians, tutors and mentors? All of them will have something to offer.

Once you've made your list, highlight or underline those people you've relied heavily on before. You've hassled them a lot – gone back to them to seek help and advice. Or are there none of these individuals whatsoever? Are you trying to do everything on your own? Are there any layers where you've consulted no one at all? Are there any untapped resources in your network?

Next, list three things you need to get done this month, and for each of the tasks, attach the name of one person who could help you to get it done quicker.

Finally, go and see them!

Note: This works the other way too. What if someone comes asking you for help? Pay it forward. Give the time. Build up an account of goodwill you can draw on when you need it.

13. Effort Activity: Looking Under the Rocks, aka Four Steps Forward

Sometimes facing the reality of a situation can seem daunting. We all hide from the facts sometimes – we know something needs changing but it can seem easier just not to make the change. Here's a good metaphor for exploring this further. Have you ever wandered down a beach and lifted up some rocks? It can be quite scary but good fun.

You never quite know what you are going to find. To begin with there seems to be no sign of life. Then you lift a rock and all sorts of squidgy creatures come out – little worms, crabs, snails, sea anemones or even the odd fish. More often than not people put the rock back down and move on, preferring not to spend too much time looking at what's underneath. But sometimes in life we have to look under the rocks to make progress.

This technique is used a lot in business. A researcher and writer called Jim Collins, in his book *Good to Great*, found that all successful companies face the brutal facts of reality, looking under the rocks for problems, even when they don't want to!

This activity is going to feel uncomfortable but by the end of it you will have a plan to make things better.

The first step is to identify any issues you think are under the rocks. This means taking some time and being really, brutally honest with yourself.

Things I need to change to improve my study at school …

The second step requires a group of four friends. Position yourself so that you are facing the group. You are then going to share your issue for change and the rest of the group are going to ask you questions and maybe offer some solutions. Listen carefully during this feedback. We quite often think that we can't change something simply because we have run out of ideas.

Now you've had a long, critical look at your progress you might be feeling pretty bruised. Take a break, go for a walk, watch TV, treat yourself to ice cream.

Once you have, it's time for the third step: time to start considering some action. What exactly can you do to improve matters?

Four Steps Forward

You might know all about origami, the Japanese art of paper folding. Those who do it can make beautiful and complex 3D models, many of which look incredible and even have moving parts. Despite these amazing constructions, the process is just a series of simple steps repeated over and over again. Every origami masterpiece begins with a single fold in a piece of paper, followed by another and another and another.

It's the same with academic learning. Sometimes we might look at a pupil who's way ahead of us and think they've achieved something impossible. But remember: all that pupil has done is execute a repeated series of steps over and over again.

For now, forget the big picture and instead concentrate on the immediate. We've found that deciding on your *next four steps* is the best way to do this.

What could you do next? Consider some of the following:

1. Calling in a favour from a friend or peer.

2. Starting a big project you've been putting off for a while.

3. Handing a piece of homework in early.

4. Rescuing a project that's behind schedule.

5. Asking five questions of a teacher to clarify a problem you've been trying to ignore.

6. Seeking a book/study guide recommendation.

7. Completing a one-hour reread and reorganise of notes on any topic.

8. Sending five emails asking for support, help, advice or an opportunity.

9. Seeing another pupil and asking them to talk you through a topic.

10. Borrowing someone else's notes.

11. Attending a support class or revision session.

12. Handing in a redone piece of work.

13. Reviewing your feedback to look for patterns.

14. Tidying your resources and summarising a topic on one sheet of A4.

OK, you've looked under the rocks and admitted a few things you aren't proud of. You've asked for extra feedback and suggestions from helpful friends. And you've considered our list of fourteen possible actions.

Now, choose the four things you're going to do and write them in the table below. Put a date next to each. And choose a reward for yourself – something you're going to do to celebrate getting your improvements underway. Make it a motivating one!

1	2	3	4	Jackpot! Reward:

6. December

The Three Phases of Practice

When pupils are working independently, what is it they are doing with their time? What specific activities are they completing – or, to put it another way, what curriculum do they design for themselves when they prepare for an exam?

We wanted to answer this question and spent time with pupils from a range of year groups asking them precisely what it was they did when they sat down to learn independently or revise for a test or exam. We ended up with a list of eighteen activities that were mentioned regularly (and a list of less common and more idiosyncratic learning methods that seemed specific to individuals). The list below represents the eighteen most common learning activities we found. We've organised them here alphabetically, not by regularity or preference.

Comparing model answers against your own work.
Completing a revision wall to display your learning.
Creating flashcards to cover what you've learned.
Creating your own exam questions.
Handing in extra exam work for marking.
Highlighting and colour coding information/notes/books.
Making and remaking class notes.
Making mind-maps, diagrams and graphic organisers.
Marking your own work to a mark scheme.
One-to-one discussions with teachers or tutors.
Planning responses to past exam questions.
Reading through class notes.
Reading through course textbooks.
Reading through model answers.
Studying mark schemes or examiners' reports.
Watching online videos and interacting with associated VLE resources.
Working with other pupils in groups/pairs to compare work.
Writing exam answers under timed conditions.

When we discussed their various approaches to independent study or revision (essentially, to practice), we found that many pupils seemed to believe that the process of revision and practice was different in each of the courses they studied. Perhaps teachers were reinforcing this or perhaps older pupils were giving this impression; whatever the source, the belief seemed to be that practice in history was different to practice in maths or French.

As we studied the results of our focus groups and discussions, we began to see that the eighteen most common activities fell into three distinct phases regardless of specific subject disciplines. It's worth considering this in relation to your own subjects. You may find that your pupils give you a different list of practice activities, but we reckon the three phases will remain the same:

» **Phase 1** activities were those that pupils completed to memorise information. We'll refer to this as the *content phase*.

» **Phase 2** activities were those that pupils chose to test themselves in high stakes conditions against the demands of the exam. This will be called the *skills phase*.

» **Phase 3** activities commonly took the work that came out of phase 2 and checked its quality in some way, identifying areas of weakness. This is the *feedback phase*.

Rearranged in these three phases, the activities look like this:

Reading through class notes.	1 – Content
Watching online videos and interacting with associated VLE resources.	1 – Content
Reading through course textbooks.	1 – Content
Making mind-maps, diagrams and graphic organisers.	1 – Content
Making and remaking class notes.	1 – Content
Highlighting and colour coding information/notes/books.	1 – Content
Creating flashcards to cover what you've learned.	1 – Content
Completing a revision wall to display your learning.	1 – Content
Writing exam answers under timed conditions.	2 – Skills
Reading through model answers.	2 – Skills
Planning responses to past exam questions.	2 – Skills
Marking your own work to a mark scheme.	3 – Feedback
Studying mark schemes or examiners' reports.	3 – Feedback
Working with other pupils in groups/pairs to compare work.	3 – Feedback
Comparing model answers against your own work.	3 – Feedback
Creating your own exam questions.	3 – Feedback
Handing in extra exam work for marking.	3 – Feedback
One-to-one discussions with teachers or tutors.	3 – Feedback

In Activity 14 we ask pupils to audit whether they use a particular technique 'always', 'sometimes' or 'never', thus giving us a sense of how they are using their time and what their conceptions of learning are. For us, there's been a very strong relationship between exam outcomes and the richness and variation of the personal curriculum the pupil designs. We've found time and again that underperforming pupils are the ones who design for themselves a very limited personal curriculum based around the repetition of only a few activities, and that this small repertoire often misses out entire phases in the practice cycle.

If you want to explain this to pupils – perhaps even to staff – this equation has been useful for us:

Knowledge = information + experience

Phase 1, the content phase, focuses purely on the acquisition and memorisation of information. Information doesn't pass exams; knowledge does. How do we forge information into knowledge? Through the experience of using that information to achieve outcomes, solve problems, construct arguments and posit answers to tricky questions. All of this happens in the skills phase. Miss out the skills phase and you remove the experiences that turn information into knowledge.

We've worked with hundreds of pupils who, for one reason or another, miss one or two of the three phases. Perhaps the descriptions below can be applied to certain types of pupil you work with.

Just Content

These pupils never move out of phase 1. Their entire independent learning curriculum focuses on memorising information. When in May you announce, 'We've covered the whole course now. We have eight lessons left to dedicate to revision, what shall we focus on?' the just content learners will ask, 'Can you do the whole course again, but really fast?' Their conception of learning is the memorisation of information.

One of two things tends to happen to these pupils as a result of this view. Some become low effort pupils because they have designed a personal curriculum with such a poverty of variation that they can't face working. We've coached pupils who only select 'always' for two or three activities, often 'reading through class notes' and 'reading through course textbooks', plus one other content activity. They look around them, see other learners putting in more hours and imagine that they too must be endlessly reading notes. It looks like a feat of super-human persistence; something they can't do. They stop working largely because they are bored.

Others become high effort pupils because they've designed a comfortable and predictable content curriculum that gives them a sense of control and removes challenge. These are the pupils who make large stationery purchases – they love their highlighters, glitter pens, flashcards and brand new notebooks. They enjoy the process of ordering and learning information, and redo it endlessly. They often become frustrated and unhappy later in the practice process when the inevitable results of their extensive labours are modest grades. 'I can't work any harder!' they say, angry at their lack of progress.

Just Content and Skills

These pupils know that good practice is more than just memorising information – there is, after all, an exam at the end of the course. Counter-intuitive as this may seem, we've worked with pupils who move through content into skills, only to stop there. They complete exam papers but don't hand them in. Since the feedback phase is the one that threatens the ego, you might find – as we did – pupils with piles of completed exams that they've hoarded rather than handed in. 'Yeah, but what if they're terrible?' they'll ask, when you encourage them to get them marked. It's an understandable response.

Just Content and Feedback

These pupils avoid the skills phase, opting instead for approaching the feedback stage as another bunch of information they're required to know. This might manifest itself

in the memorisation of mark schemes, for example, so they know the precise descriptor for an A* without having attempted to build an A* answer themselves. They might know which topics have appeared in which exam and in which order over the last five years, having memorised the structure of the papers without completing any of them. They might bury their heads in examiners' reports as a proxy for taking an actual exam.

Because they've missed the skills phase, their understanding is only theoretical, so these are the pupils who have a meltdown if the wording of the paper deviates in the slightest from what is expected. If the exam requires the learner to comment on 'gender roles' instead of 'the presentation of men and women', the content and feedback pupil can't function. In the end, their lack of experience undoes them.

Only by spending time in all three phases can pupils practise effectively. December is a good time to audit current approaches and encourage pupils to change because they have sufficient content to be able to test themselves, even if it's in small chunks. Watch out for the just content pupil who tells you they can't attempt an exam paper until they've memorised the entire course; high practice pupils take exams in small chunks, attempting a six-marker or a twelve-marker in isolation, then seeking feedback.

Here's the questionnaire, adapted from our first book, *The A Level Mindset*.

14. Practice Activity: The Practice Questionnaire

We've found there is a strong link between the kind of revision someone does and the outcomes they get. So, which pupil will do better in an exam?

» Pupil 1 does fifteen hours of revision – all of it reading through class notes.

» Pupil 2 only does ten hours of revision – two hours making mind-maps, two hours creating flashcards of key terms, three hours writing timed essays, two hours working through past papers and looking for patterns in the questions asked, and half an hour doing the hardest question they could find, followed by half an hour talking it through with their teacher. Then they spend five hours shopping with their friends and watching TV.

You too can make less mean more. Try this questionnaire:

Name: _____   Subject: _____

1 How many hours of independent work do you do on your subjects outside of class? Please state the time spent on each subject.

2 What sort of activities do you do? Use the table below:

		Always	Sometimes	Never
Reading through class notes	C			
Using resources on the school's VLE	C			
Using course textbooks	C			
Mind-maps/diagrams	C			
Making/remaking class notes	C			
Highlighting/colour coding	C			
Flashcards	C			
Using a revision wall to display your learning	C			
Writing exam answers under timed conditions	S			
Reading model answers	S			
Using past exam questions and planning answers	S			
Marking your own work to a mark scheme	F			

Studying mark schemes or examiners' reports	F			
Working with other pupils in groups/pairs	F			
Comparing model answers against your own work	F			
Creating your own exam questions	F			
Handing in extra exam work for marking	F			
One-to-one discussions with teachers/tutors	F			

3 Additional activities not mentioned above:

4 Write a brief account of what you do if you can't understand something (e.g. try again, read textbooks, check the school's VLE, see teachers, see other pupils).

You will notice some activities have a 'C' next to them – these are the *content* techniques. Some activities have an 'S' next to them – these are the *skills* techniques. Others have an 'F' next to them – these are the *feedback* techniques.

Notice in our example that pupil 1 only does content revision, while pupil 2 does all three stages and then takes some time off. In our experience, pupil 2 will pretty much always get a better grade than pupil 1. And they put in fewer hours.

Have a look at the activities associated with each stage of revision and draw up a list of three or four you aren't doing at the moment but that you'd like to try:

1.

2.

3.

4.

15. Effort Activity: The Three 'Hows' of Independent Work

We've worked with thousands of pupils who are great at designing revision; they create amazing revision and independent work plans that fill every minute of the day, but then just don't follow through on the plan.

It's something we've all done; if you have too, don't beat yourself up about it. Why do we procrastinate? Why do we avoid putting the effort in?

This might surprise you, but saying that you are going to do some 'independent work' or 'revision' is actually part of the problem. When you say that you are going to revise (as far as your brain is concerned), it's vague and ambiguous. When your brain thinks that you are about to do something that's vague and ambiguous it will often start to come up with reasons why you shouldn't do it (which can be quite useful). This probably sounds a bit odd, but your brain starts thinking that this isn't really a well thought out plan. It's not sure what you are going to be doing, or how, and your brain starts to get you thinking that it might not even work. Then you procrastinate.

So how do you get past this?

It's quite a simple strategy but we promise you it works. You have to get specific. Here's how. Before every independent work session or revision session you have to sit down and answer these three questions:

1 **How am I going to revise/work?** Here you have to be specific about the *how* (what strategy you are going to use) and also *what* you are going to revise. This means identifying specifically the topics you are going to cover and the activities you're going to do to cover the work.

2 **How long am I going to revise/work for?** Be very clear about the time. If you are doing active revision this shouldn't be any longer than two hours. Remember to build in short (ten minute) breaks every forty minutes. Use Twenty-Five Minute Sprints (Activity 26) to help structure sessions and it becomes even easier to beat procrastination.

3 **How will I know if I've made progress?** How are you going to test yourself? If you just sit for two hours passively reading your notes you will have no idea if you have made any progress, so you'll need to test yourself in some way. It might be a set of

questions you answer, a mini-lecture that you give to yourself or short-answer questions you're going to do under timed conditions towards the end of the session.

You can get into the habit of doing this mentally, but to start with complete the table below before you start every independent work or revision session. Then start!

How am I going to revise/work?	
How long am I going to revise/ work for?	
How will I know if I've made progress?	

16. Practice Activity: It's Time to Teach, aka CASTT

Cal Newport is a professor of computer science at Georgetown University, Washington, DC. He's written a few great books to help pupils achieve the best grades they can. It's worth taking a look at his website: www.calnewport.com.

In addition to teaching pupils at university, he's been fascinated by the strategies pupils use to help them get great grades. He suggests that when it comes to revision there are two types: active recall and passive recall.

» Active recall is *actively trying to understand and synthesise the information by teaching it.* (Don't worry, you don't need your own class of Year 7s for this! You can do it alone or to someone else – a friend, a parent or a sibling.)

» Passive recall, by contrast, is just sitting passively reading your notes.

Newport makes a bold statement: *active recall is the only revision strategy that counts*! He argues that there are three huge benefits to this type of super-charged revision:

1. It's very effective.

2. It saves time.

3. It's difficult and mentally uncomfortable. (Don't worry, it's supposed to be!)

So how do you do it?

We've set a little challenge for you. We want you to *only* use active recall for the next test you have in one of your subjects. During this time you are not allowed to use any other strategy. You are either doing active recall or preparing for it. No sitting comfortably and reading your notes!

If you're interested in trying this experiment, you'll need to start about three weeks before a test or mock exam and you'll need to set aside a few hours each week. Block the time out on your planner before you start, then follow our CASTT process.

Week 1: Collect and Arrange (C and A)

This week is preparation week – we call it 'collect and arrange' because it gives you a chance to gather everything you need and make sense of it. The first thing you need to do is identify and collect the topics you will be tested on – make a list of them. A syllabus might help here or a list provided by a teacher. Once you've got your list of topics, you're really in business. You know the size of the job ahead of you.

Once you've identified and collected together your topics, you need to arrange or organise your notes for the topics. Try to condense the material into a small space – one or two sides of A4, for example. It might be useful to use mind-maps for this or other graphic organisers like tables, lists, bullet points or flow charts. Consider trying one of our faves – a Nine-Box Grid (Activity 27).

Weeks 2 and 3: Search (S) and Teach (T)

Now you'll need to do a search for any past paper questions connected to the topics you've collected and arranged in week 1. You're trying to find examples that are as close to the one you're going to encounter in the test coming up – in other words, to reproduce the test experience! Search everywhere. Do you already have exam questions in your books or folders? Did your teachers hand some out? Are there some on your school's online resources or in the school library? Maybe an exam board website can help. You want to be the person who has searched out more exam questions than anyone else!

Once you've got your hoard, you can begin teaching – in other words, it's active recall only! Grab your exam question, write it in the middle of a sheet of A4 and plan an answer around it. Now, imagine you're a teacher, explaining how to answer the question to your class. Assume that this class need things to be explained really slowly and clearly, and you're at the front with a whiteboard, explaining exactly *what to do, how to do it* and *why to do it*.

In week 2 it might be that you try to teach the information with only yourself present. Have the mind-map in front of you and aim to recall and explain as much information as possible without looking. It might be useful to cover up your mind-map and then just expose sections if you are struggling. Don't worry if it's not perfect – it won't be at first. Remember that you have to speak out loud. It will feel odd at first but just keep going.

In week 3 you might try teaching with an audience. Give someone the mind-map while you try to recall. Get the observer to make a note of anything you miss. Then try it again.

Test (T)

Finally, to check that the process is working effectively, you must test yourself. Put away all the mind-maps and notes from weeks 1, 2 and 3, clear your desk and put your phone on airplane settings. Now, write a response to the exam question under timed conditions.

Take it to a teacher for marking or check it against a mark scheme.

And that's it! Active recall in four steps. It might not always feel easy or relaxed, but it's quick, intense and effective. Remember CASTT next time you need to practise for a test or exam!

17. Vision Activity: Setting a Personal Best

You've probably heard of setting a personal best (PB) before. It's a term often used in the sporting world to explain when an athlete records their best ever time. It's something most athletes are always striving for – to push beyond a time or distance they've achieved before in an event. Quite often the goal is just to beat their last time or distance by a fraction of a second or a centimetre. The gains are usually small but make a big difference.

Professor Andrew Martin (2011) at the University of Sydney has used this strategy with pupils and found that it can make a big difference to academic performance.

So how does it work?

There are three important things about PBs. First, they are personal. That means *you* have to decide what the target is going to be. You can ask your teacher for advice, but ultimately it's about you deciding what you'd like to go for.

Second, you need to be specific. You can't set a target that isn't specific or you won't know when you've achieved a PB. So, it might be that you set a PB for specific homework, perhaps a percentage grade that you want to achieve that's better than you've had before.

Third, you need just the right level of challenge. This means pushing yourself out of your comfort zone (see the diagram below) and into your learning zone. Be careful not to push yourself into the panic zone. You want a PB that will stretch you but it must be achievable. You can always go for another PB once you've achieved this new level.

Getting the level of challenge right

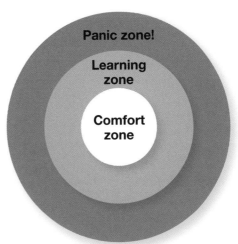

Panic zone!

Learning zone

Comfort zone

Finally, use the table below to set your PB. An example has been done for you.

Challenge (What's the goal?)	Current score (What's the best score you've achieved?)	PB target (What's the target for your new PB?)
To get my best ever score in a GCSE maths paper	67%	70%

18. Vision Activity: Success Leaves Clues

Who's already done what you want to do?

Jim Rohn said that 'success leaves clues'. What he meant by this is that you can learn from other people who have already done what you'd like to do. There are millions of pupils who have already taken their GCSEs and millions of these pupils will have done really well. You'll probably find these pupils have some very good advice. It's crazy that we don't spend more time learning from people who have already been through what we would like to do and learning from their mistakes. The message is that we don't have to make the same mistakes!

So what did they do?

This activity involves you speaking to a pupil who has already done well in their GCSEs and maybe some pupils who didn't. This might be something that your teacher can arrange for you or you might be able to ask a friend's older brother or sister.

You'll need about fifteen minutes to do this activity. It might feel a bit awkward, but just think of yourself as a journalist trying to find out a story of success. You'll need a pen, paper and maybe a copy of the questions below. When you start the conversation, it will be worth writing down the answers or recording the conversation on your phone so you can listen to it later.

You could start the conversation by asking some of the following questions:

» What is your dream job?

» What do you hope to achieve by completing your A levels/BTEC/apprenticeship?

» What obstacles do you think you may have to overcome while at school?

» How many hours a week of independent study did you do for your GCSEs?

» Describe a typical hour of your revision.

» In an average week, how many hours did you spend on homework?

» How did you decide what you needed to revise?

» What did you do with the work you got back?

» If you did past paper questions, did you ever self-mark them?

» What revision materials did you use/produce?

» What did you do when you encountered a problem?

» How did you respond to setbacks?

» What was your response to a poor grade in a test or homework?

» What advice would you give your Year 10 self when first starting your GCSEs?

When you've finished the interview (it would be useful to do a few), identify what you think are the key points and write them in the table below. Try to get ten points for each column and then keep this visible in your study area at home.

What do successful pupils do?	What do pupils who haven't been successful do?

7. January

Agency and Efficacy

January is a difficult month. The mornings are dark and cold, mock exam results have often delivered a disappointing kicking and the summer seems a long way off. Even the most dedicated pupil can feel low. It's important to distinguish between those learners who, despite feeling gloomy, have established positive habits and behaviours and those who are totally floored. This is the month in which you go all out to try to rescue the latter – the low attitude pupils.

When we use the term 'low attitude' to describe a learner, we're describing listless, fixed mindset pupils with fast vanishing levels of self-belief. We've discovered (again, it seems pretty obvious in hindsight) that you can't cheerlead these low attitude pupils. If you've got a cohort beset with fears of the future and paralysed by a crisis of self-belief, leading a cheery assembly won't be enough to lift them. Assertions that 'You can do it! Everything's going to be great!' don't work with low attitude youngsters.

Why not? We've done a lot of work on this topic, working with low attitude pupils, making a careful note of our successes and failures and reading a huge amount of educational research. Reflecting on our more recent work with pupils we've begun to see subdivisions of attitude emerge.

We've found the following terms helpful in January. We hope you do too:

» **Agency**: the pupil's perception of their ability to directly control or influence the course of their life.

» **Efficacy**: the pupil's perception of their capability to successfully execute a particular task or challenge.

Coaching conversations that place an emphasis on these terms, rather than on self-esteem (the pupil's sense of their own worth as a person) might yield better results. We reckon a useful argument could be built that increases in agency and efficacy lead to a respective increase in self-esteem. Go at self-esteem via the others, rather than starting there.

Agency

Pupils with low levels of agency think life is happening *to* them. Those with higher levels of agency think life is happening *for* them.

Let's examine this more closely. Pupils with a low sense of their own agency feel like pinballs buffeted around in someone else's game. If you listen to them talk, they might actually use metaphors about games of chance. 'These are the cards I've been dealt,' they might say or think. They're fatalistic. They don't believe in their ability to control their chaotic and random lives. Plans just get blown away by fate. Those who carve out

lives they love are just lucky, thinks this pupil; the rest of us just have to live with whatever emerges. So if you present these pupils with an opportunity – let's say the chance to apply for a place at a summer school – they won't bother. Stuff like that happens to other people, they think. These pupils are stuck in an unenviable place: they're going to be held accountable for their GCSE results, yet they feel they have no control over them.

Pupils with a higher sense of agency think life is happening for them. They're not entitled – the world doesn't owe these pupils a living – they're just confident enough to tune in to the host of chances and opportunities out there. They see the extra classes and lunchtime revision sessions as a chance to clarify errors and fill gaps in knowledge. If things go wrong – and they go wrong for pupils with a higher sense of agency the same number of times and in just as many ways as they do for other pupils – they may feel down about it, but their conception of the world still encourages them to look for learning opportunities. They get up and try again. 'Maybe I can learn something from this,' they eventually conclude, before making another plan.

We're fond of using a section of Dr Tina Seelig's excellent *inGenius: A Crash Course on Creativity* to illustrate this point to pupils. Seelig teaches a course on creativity at Harvard and tells the following story. Her course is very popular and one particular year the teaching team had to whittle the class down from 150 to 40. Following the application process decisions were made. Later, Seelig received a note from a pupil who hadn't made it on to the course. 'He said that he *never* gets into the courses he wants,' Seelig writes. 'I thought carefully about how to respond and sent him the following message: "If there is a course you really want to take and you don't get a spot in the class, then just keep showing up. Spots usually open up during the first week as pupils drop the class for a variety of reasons. If you're there, you're almost guaranteed the spot."' Seelig got a reply: 'Thank you for this advice. I assume that won't work for your class.' Seelig writes, 'I stared at his e-mail for several minutes and then responded, "Yes, you're right. It won't work." I had handed him the ruby slippers and he didn't take them.' Seelig contrasts this with a second pupil whose application was also unsuccessful, but who wrote to ask if she could attend just one class having enjoyed the application task. When a pupil dropped out a week later, she got the place. Seelig concludes: 'These two students are both intelligent. The difference between them is their attitude. The first fellow … didn't even see the possibility when I placed it in front of him. The second student created a way to get what she wanted' (Seelig, 2012, p. 169–170).

Efficacy

A neat experiment run by Barry Zimmerman at New York University in the early eighties summarises efficacy – the pupil's sense of their capability – with helpful clarity. Zimmerman and Ringle (1981) gave kids an impossible challenge (untangling a knot of wires) and an adult to model the process of problem solving before giving them a go too. One group got a pessimistic adult: 'I don't think I can separate these wires,' they said after a period of trying. 'I've tried many different ways and nothing seems to work.' The other group got an optimistic adult who, experiencing struggle, said things like, 'I'm sure I can separate these wires; I just have to keep trying different ways and then I'll find the right one.' Of course, pupils in this second group (despite being no more successful than the others) reported higher levels of efficacy and, as a result, persisted for longer.

Here, the level of efficacy had been determined by seeing others attempt the task, something Albert Bandura (1997) calls efficacy formed through 'vicarious experiences'. It might be helpful to take a moment to look at Bandura's efficacy model. He argues that the four major influences on a pupil's level of efficacy are: (1) task performance (the perceived level of success in a subject, grades and type of feedback), (2) vicarious experiences like the one described above, usually coming via pupil work or class demonstrations, (3) verbal persuasion (the focus the teacher's intervention and feedback places on practical adjustments to the task, possible solutions and the importance of effort) and (4) psychological state (emotional response to pressure, anxiety and fear of failure).

If you want to measure a pupil's levels of efficacy, perhaps as the starting point for a coaching conversation, a good place to start is with the work of Schwarzer and Jerusalem (1995) whose simple ten-question questionnaire gives a score between 10 and 40:

1 I can always manage to solve difficult problems if I try hard enough.

2 If someone opposes me, I can find the means and ways to get what I want.

3 It is easy for me to stick to my aims and accomplish my goals.

4 I am confident that I could deal efficiently with unexpected events.

5 Thanks to my resourcefulness, I know how to handle unforeseen situations.

6 I can solve most problems if I invest the necessary effort.

7 I can remain calm when facing difficulties because I can rely on my coping abilities.

8 When I am confronted with a problem, I can usually find several solutions.

9 If I am in trouble, I can usually think of a solution.

10 I can usually handle whatever comes my way.

For each statement, assign a number from the following rating scale: 1 = not at all true, 2 = hardly true, 3 = moderately true or 4 = exactly true.

One of the keys to helping pupils with low levels of efficacy, and therefore boosting the learner's persistence, is explored in research undertaken by Margolis and McCabe (2006, p. 225) who recommend that teachers, tutors and coaches 'attribute failure to controllable factors … and modifiable abilities'. In other words, at a difficult time of year like January, solution focused feedback and practical, supported problem solving beats motivational speeches.

Coaches, Not Cheerleaders

In January, pupils need coaching rather than cheerleading. For us, that means beginning with a calm and clear emphasis on the goal for the final five months. There are two vision activities to help you do this. The attitude activities in this chapter aim to give pupils the feeling of control, of agency and efficacy. Of course, you'll be working with pupils who don't feel in control as well as those with more psychological and emotional resources,

so you'll be observing their differing reactions to the problems and changes ahead.
The challenge for Key Stage 4 tutors is to convince young people of their agency and to empower as many of them as you can.

19. Vision Activity: Five Roads

In this simple activity, all you need to do is imagine yourself at a crossroads with five possible ways forward: each way forward represents a possible choice for you. The aim of this activity is to make those choices clearer. That way you can objectively review your options, which is the first step in making a good decision. Don't feel a decision has to be made yet – it doesn't. But knowing what options are in play is always helpful.

Use the diagram below to think about what might lie at the end of each road and scribble some notes at the tip of each one. Make the notes as detailed as you can.

You might need to spend some time thinking about these. It may well be a good idea to begin by putting two or three options at the end of each road and coming back to add more or cross others off as your preferences become clearer …

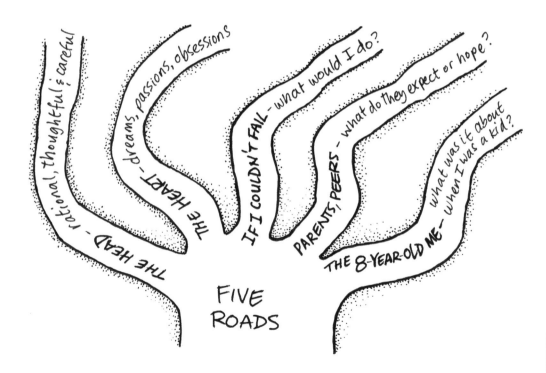

THE HEAD – rational, thoughtful & careful

THE HEART – dreams, passions, obsessions

IF I COULDN'T FAIL – what would I do?

PARENTS, PEERS – what do they expect or hope?

THE 8-YEAR-OLD ME – what was it about when I was a kid?

FIVE ROADS

» **The head.** Here, note down the choices that occur to you when you think rationally. This is the careful and thoughtful road. There will be low risk on this road – it's safe and certain – so it might not be your most exciting road forward.

» **The heart.** This road is about wholeheartedly pursuing your passions; the stuff that makes you excited and that you would willingly spend time on for free. This might be a riskier road, with greater levels of uncertainty, but you'll be fired up as well as slightly fearful as you travel it!

» **If I couldn't fail.** At the end of this imaginary road is guaranteed success in something. It will be a hard road to travel, and there may be tough times, but it will end in 100% success. In other words, if you knew you couldn't fail at something, what would you choose to do?

» **Parents, peers.** Here, you consider what others are expecting of you. You may be surrounded by people with strong opinions – teachers, tutors, parents and extended family – all telling you that you have to pursue something or that you're a natural at something. You might, or might not, agree with them. Make a note of all the things you feel a pressure to pursue here.

» **The 8-year-old me.** If you'd done this activity in primary school, what would you have said you wanted to do in the future? Often, we find that elements of our early passions persist; you might write something down here and suddenly remember a passion that you've forgotten or forced yourself to ignore. Maybe it's time to revisit it, or maybe there are just parts of it that are still relevant today.

Once you've got some ideas scribbled at the end of each road, let these thoughts develop for a few days. Consider returning to this activity more than once as the year goes on, adjusting your responses each time.

Finally: don't feel you need to make a decision yet. Just knowing the possible ways forward puts you in a strong position. And when you travel a road, it doesn't mean you can never return and change direction. You can!

20. Vision Activity: The Ten-Year Grid

We've based this activity on one proposed by Alison and David Price in their book *Psychology of Success, A Practical Guide* (2011), which we thoroughly recommend! Have a look at the grid below. It's a 20 x 26 grid with 520 little boxes in it. Each box represents a week of your life for the next ten years.

Now ask yourself what you want your life to be like in ten years' time. You don't have to be super-specific. Try to make notes under the following headings:

» A job that involves …

» Places I've enjoyed visiting, including …

» Friends and family I value because they …

» A lifestyle that allows me to …

This grid represents the weeks you've got to achieve all that.

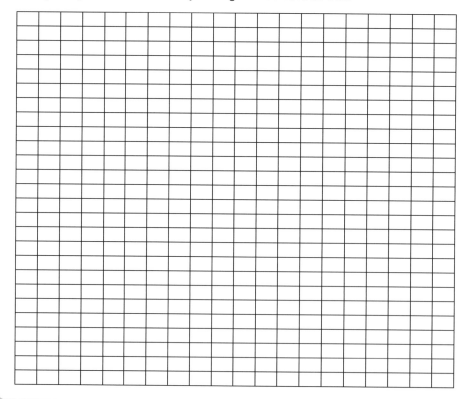

Looking at it this way, ten years doesn't seem quite as much time. And it gets more alarming … Before you begin, shade out the following:

» **Sleep: six full columns.** Assuming just under eight hours a night, that's all the time in the next ten years that you'll be asleep – about 33% of the time!

» **Leisure and 'trapped time': five full columns.** We've gone to the Office for National Statistics for this one. After analysing lifestyles, they conclude that we spend about 6% of our time during mealtimes, about 11% of our time watching TV, 6% of our time travelling from one place to another and 2% of our time on 'personal care' (brushing teeth, make-up, shaving, etc.). That's about 25% of the next ten years you'll be using up.

So, in total you have to clear eleven of the twenty columns. That's over half your time!

Now how many weeks have you got left to build that life for yourself? 234. And that's assuming you want it to happen in ten years; secretly, you might really want it sooner. And there are other things that you haven't shaded off – school, family time and other commitments that remove blocks from the grid.

The conclusion: whatever it is you want to achieve, if you want it soon, *you need to get started.*

But before you do …

The Power of Negative Visualisation

Think about your vision for a life ten years from now. Crazy as it sounds, the chances are that many of the obstacles you'll need to overcome won't come from external circumstances. They will come from *you*. You'll put obstacles in the way of your own potential happiness. In *Rethinking Positive Thinking* (2014), the psychologist Gabrielle Oettingen argues that we all have this tendency to sabotage our own success. But by confronting the obstacles we put in our own way – by visualising them blocking our progress – we get better at removing them.

Is there a part of your personality that might compromise your potential success? An element of your personality you need to watch out for? Obstacles you might actually put in your own way?

Imagine that, for one of the reasons you've thought about, you take no action towards your goal.

Let's imagine you've just visualised an exciting life for yourself ten years from now, put this book down, and you've found, after a busy week, that you've taken no action. Shade out one week of your grid.

Now imagine another month has passed – a busy month with lots going on – and you still haven't managed to get started. Shade out four more of your boxes. As you do this, try to put yourself in the shoes of the future you. With a month gone by, how is this feeling?

What if Christmas comes around and you haven't been able to find the time or energy to take any action? That's three months. Shade out twelve of your boxes. Again, try to connect with the feelings you might experience if this really happens.

A whole year is two full columns. Visualise a year having passed and, for whatever reason, you haven't yet managed to take any action. Scratch two columns. How would you be feeling if that really did happen?

Now look further ahead. How will you feel if three years on – that's six full columns – you haven't done anything?

This negative visualisation might help you. Whenever time passes without you taking action, return to this grid and watch the weeks disappearing.

Then get yourself back on track!

21. Attitude Activity: The Battery

Dr Steve Bull was the England and Wales cricket team's psychologist for seventeen years, working with players who experienced huge pressure to perform day in, day out. As a result, he has developed a series of interesting tools for boosting people's confidence in their own ability. In his book, *The Game Plan* (2006, p. 33), Bull says, 'It seems to be a human frailty that we are programmed to focus on failure and disappointment far more than on success and accomplishment. We find it very easy to recall those disastrous days when everything went wrong.' He goes on to say that 'When we are faced with a similar challenge, our brains are quick to recall the previous catastrophe.' He then concludes that 'the cycle must be broken, and the most effective way of doing this is to actively reconnect your mind with previous accomplishments'. Dr Bull worked with cricketers asking them to record their previous successes, and saw their confidence rocket and their performances improve as a result.

Bull uses mountain peaks as his confidence metaphor, but we prefer the image of a phone battery. We like the idea of a battery because confidence in your ability gives you energy. It charges you up and fills you with strength and belief. You can keep your battery topped up by recalling those times when things went brilliantly and you really achieved what you were capable of.

You have five energy slots to fill. Your job is to fill each slot with a brief description of a time when you performed really well and achieved something you are pleased with or proud of. When you're feeling low, you can return to your battery, read the information there and feel yourself recharge with positivity and purpose.

But what do you write in the five slots? Try using the following as guidelines:

» Times when you supported or helped someone perform better or taught them something.

» Times when your family members valued you for doing the right thing, making a good decision or doing a good turn.

» Times when you worked in a team, adding value to that team.

» Times when you did something you felt scared about, facing down your fear.

» Times when you performed well in a test or a homework and got a grade/score you were pleased with.

» Times when you made a difficult decision.

» Times when your strengths, skills and talents meant you did a good job.

» Times you've been rewarded – either verbally through someone saying thank you, or via a letter home, a certificate or an award.

Go back as far as you can. A well-charged confidence battery draws on achievements from all areas of your life and from all times of your life, so don't limit yourself to school or this academic year. You've been doing good work for a long time now – think hard to recall it all!

22. Systems Activity: The Bottom Left

Sometimes the number of jobs you have to do can be overwhelming. Teachers are making demands from all angles and it's difficult to know where to start. The trouble with listing jobs is that a list doesn't allow you to see the bigger picture; you can't assess the progress of whole projects, you can only pick off small individual tasks.

Using a matrix or a grid helps you to assess the status of entire subjects. And once you've got a good sense of how an entire subject is going, you can use your time much more effectively, targeting your energy where it's most needed.

Put every subject you study onto this grid:

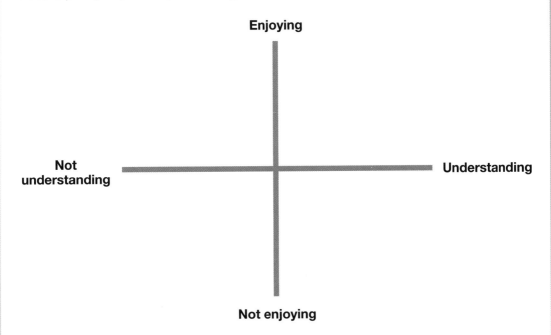

Once you've made these decisions and placed these projects as dots or crosses on the grid, make notes under each dot explaining the reasons why you've positioned it there. Then have a look at the projects in the bottom left of the grid.

The Terror of the Bottom Left!

Many pupils will subconsciously avoid the subjects in the bottom left because even the thought of them feels uncomfortable. They might lower the standards they expect of themselves in those subjects, work less hard at them or try to ignore them altogether. But they're not going to go away. By spending some time on them now you could avoid a real crisis later on in the year.

For each bottom left subject make a note of:

» One task you could do that will push the dot further to the right.

» One task you could do that will push the dot further upwards.

It might be speaking to a teacher, borrowing some missing work, attending an after-school class, speaking to a pupil who's better at it than you, finishing reading a textbook or redoing a rushed piece of homework.

Good prioritisation means knowing *why you're doing what you're doing*. This task will help you to focus on your weaknesses.

23. Attitude Activity: Managing Reactions to Feedback

Our response to getting feedback can vary considerably. Some people are hungry for feedback and want to know how they can improve; others avoid feedback like the plague and take it personally. If you want to get good grades at GCSE you are going to have to get comfortable with feedback. Steve Bull, in his brilliant book *The Game Plan* (2006, p. 125), has developed an acronym, SADRAA, to help you with the process. He suggests that when you get feedback you might not be happy with, you should work through three stages: the red zone, the blue zone and the green zone.

The table below explains the zones. Low performing pupils can sometimes get caught up in the red zone and some might never leave. You might know people like this! It's fine to have these initial emotions, of course, but then you must push through the next two stages.

The red zone Emotions	**S**hock	Wow – I did not expect that! I'm really surprised by those comments.
	Anger	How dare they say that! That teacher has never liked me. Wait till I get my own back.
	Denial	I'm not like that at all. That's totally wrong.
The blue zone Thinking	**R**ationalisation	OK, maybe it seems true from their perspective. But the reason they think that is because they don't know what kind of pressure I'm under. Anyway, that's the way I am and why should I change? And even if I wanted to, how could I?
The green zone Behaviour	**A**cceptance	OK, maybe I need to change something. Maybe I could look at a few different ways of doing things to see if they improve matters.
	Action	Right, what do I need to do?

The next time that you have some feedback that you might not be happy with, use the table below to either record your own thoughts or check in with your emotional response to the criticism and see which zone you're in. Then look ahead to the next zone and see what kind of thoughts you might try to have to move yourself through the process more quickly. Ultimately, you'll be much happier if you avoid getting stuck in the red or blue zone!

It might be tricky to get to the green zone, so feel free to leave it a day or so – maybe longer – before completing the final box or considering the ideas you see there.

The zones	Your thoughts ...
The red zone Emotions	
The blue zone Thinking	
The green zone Behaviour	

8. February

Effort is Relative

Low effort pupils have been on every teacher's radar from the start, of course, but February is one of those moments, post-mock exam results, where it becomes staggeringly clear which learners haven't yet made a change in the levels of effort and commitment to their studies. We still feel a kind of stressed out tightening of the stomach and a prickle of sweat on the brow as we count up the number of kids whose effort levels are still way off where they need to be.

When it comes to making concerted, cohort wide attempts to raise levels of effort, we've made a whole bunch of mistakes it might be useful to share here. When we began our research eight years ago courses were modular. We used to interview pupils who'd had a terrible Year 10 or first half of Year 11, or in sixth form the Year 12s, looking for the weaknesses that had resulted in their underperformance. One of the questions we'd ask is, 'How hard have you worked this year?' Often, pupils couldn't give us specifics. 'On a scale of 1–10,' we'd add for clarification. We were looking for a neat and tidy admission along the lines of, 'I'd estimate a 2, nowhere near hard enough. I should've done so much more!' that we could then share with others. But we didn't get it. Pupils who'd had a hugely disappointing year, or were in the midst of a poor period of results, would give us much higher scores for effort.

Most common were 5 or 6. We got these responses over and over again. It didn't make sense.

We were making a ludicrous error. Looking back, we should have seen it earlier. Perceptions of effort are relative. Low effort pupils don't know they're low effort pupils. They know they're not high, but they're convinced they're only a matter of a few hours beneath the top performers. In other words, in their minds they're a 5 or 6.

That's why low effort pupils aren't perturbed by their levels of effort. For many of them, the work they're doing for you now represents the hardest they've ever worked. These are pupils who have cruised through Years 8 and 9 dashing off homework at the last minute, winging their way through tests and exams, and just about surviving. They're used to maybe two hours of reactive independent study per week.

They've upped their game and now they're completing three or four hours a week – close to double what they've done before. They're feeling good about the way things are going, and they've taken steps to reinforce that feeling of comfort by establishing peer groups composed of pupils whose effort levels are similar. Low effort pupils make friends with low effort pupils, normalising their four hours a week. They cannot spend any meaningful time with high effort pupils,

of course, or they'll shatter their convenient and comfortable worldview. This can be a painful process. Low effort pupils, when first introduced to the habits and routines of high effort pupils, will deny them. We've had intervention conversations with low effort pupils, together with their parents, during which the pupil has claimed, 'But no one is working as hard as that!' or 'The teachers say we should be working hard, but no one listens!' When you're a pupil who has carefully chosen a peer group of low effort friends, it really can seem as though the whole world is ignoring the advice of the organisation. The reality can be very different.

So how can we turn low effort pupils into high effort pupils?

The answer is: one week at a time. It's a slow and steady process of gradually incremented steps. Hundreds of interventions and coaching conversations with low effort pupils have led us to the following model.

Phase 1: Habitualise Six Hours a Week

(Time taken – three weeks)

Habit formation requires a reminder (a time, place or event that serves as a trigger), a routine (a repeated action, i.e. a chunk of concentrated study) and a reward. We've had success sharing this with pupils and leading habit formation sessions where pupils commit to a new way of doing things by selecting each of their three R's. (There's a specific activity in *The A Level Mindset* called The Three R's of Habit – check it out.)

Low effort pupils have no current routines and find it hard to create new ones. They've spent the last three or four years in reactive mode. (They wait for instruction. The work gets done once the work has been set – and who knows when that will be?) So they need help frameworking their new proactive habit.

Here's where you might begin:

Reminder: 3.30pm

Routine: One hour and fifteen minutes of activity in a quiet place, finishing at 4.45pm, broken into the following three sections:

1. *Twenty-five minutes of high intensity work with no distractions and your phone on airplane settings.*

2. *Twenty-five minutes off. Relaxing, catching up, checking social media, listening to music, etc.*

3. *Twenty-five minutes on again: super-intense, no distractions whatsoever.*

Reward: Whatever the pupil chooses, within reason – a TV programme, a blast of music, a cuppa and a biscuit.

If you can get this to happen for a full week, the pupil will have done close to six hours (excluding the twenty-five minute breaks, of course). Certainly, it will be the hardest working week they'll have done for some time. They'll feel hit for six.

More importantly, though, they'll struggle to fill these six intense hours. These are learners who have grown adept at dashing off pieces of work as quickly and effortlessly as they can. So they'll tell you there just isn't enough work being set to justify six hours of independent study.

The answer is probably not to ask teaching staff to set more work. (It may be. If you feel your organisation is genuinely asking far too little of its learners, there's a challenge ahead and you'll need the support of senior leaders.) Instead, the answer might well be to draw up a list of high effort activities that your best pupils are already choosing to do in their study time – you're gathering leading indicators here. Get a focus group together and ask them. Pick the most replicable. If your list is anything like ours, it will have these kinds of things on it:

» Checking the organisation and legibility of notes. Going through them to highlight key points.

» Creating glossaries of key definitions with examples.

» Thematically organising the learning so far using a range of possible graphic organisers (e.g. mind-maps, charts, tables, diagrams, lists).

» Using course textbooks or your VLE to reinforce and then extend learning.

» Auditing feedback so far to make a hit list of common errors and areas for improvement.

» Comparing model answers against their own work and making a list of commitments for next time.

These are tasks that high effort pupils set themselves. Low effort pupils will consider this entirely lunatic (why would anyone *voluntarily set themselves work*?), but you can slowly habitualise these routines. When reviewing the week, ask the pupils what they did with their fifty minutes of study, and return to your list of high effort activities to further challenge and support habit formation.

Phase 2: Habitualise Nine Hours a Week

(Time taken – another three weeks)

Here's where you might go next:

Reminder: *3.30pm*

Routine: *One hour and thirty minutes of activity in a quiet place, finishing at 5pm, broken into the following five sections:*

1. *Twenty-five minutes of high intensity work with no distractions and your phone on airplane settings.*

2. *Five minutes off. Time for a quick check of social media, one tune, a stretch or a walk.*

3. *Twenty-five minutes on again: super-intense, no distractions whatsoever.*

4. *Five minutes off.*

5. *Twenty-five minutes on again: same as above – intense and focused.*

Reward: *Again, whatever the pupil chooses, within reason.*

If you can get this to happen for a full week, the pupil will have done close to nine hours, excluding mini-breaks. This is a significant step forward. Some of the pupils you intervene with might not ever get this far, but if they do, they're putting in levels of effort that will reap real rewards.

A word on timings: the examples above assume an after-school session of some description. (Not always necessary, though we're big fans of 'period 6'!) If the option is not there for you, try modelling the process once or twice, then hand over responsibility to the pupil by shifting the start time to 4.30pm and requiring that they do it at home. With some cohorts we've set up a room for a pre-school session starting at 7.30am and finishing just as the day begins, or run shorter lunchtime sessions.

Rewards and the 'Sustaining Expectations Effect'

We've come across an interesting issue using this method of intervention, particularly when working with pupils who had previously been openly low effort, disengaged or disruptive.

This is what happens. Teachers, when informed of the intervention, will understandably express their frustration ('Getting yet another chance, is he?' 'They're lazy. There's nothing you can do about it.' 'I think you're wasting your time giving extra support to this one.'). The Pygmalion effect has been extensively studied in education (starting with Rosenthal and Jacobson in 1968) – that is, the tendency for expectations of pupil behaviour to create it. One study from the University of Grenoble summarises Pygmalion constructs well, describing how the models, 'usually consist of three stages: (i) teachers develop expectations for pupils' future achievement, (ii) they treat pupils differently according to these expectations, (iii) this differential treatment influences, directly or indirectly … the pupils' achievement' (Trouilloud et al., 2002, p. 594).

We've seen pupils in the early stages of a concerted effort to change return to us despondent. They've tried to increase their levels of effort, their story goes, but no one's noticed. Teachers haven't been supportive; there's been no positive feedback or encouragement, no sign of progress whatsoever. Often they've received the opposite in the form of a dubious look, a roll of the eyes, a humorous or wry comment. Cooper and Good (1983) call this the 'sustaining expectations effect', something they argue occurs (the italics here are ours) 'when pupil performance is sustained at a pre-existing level because of teacher expectations … teachers respond on the basis of their *existing expectations for pupils* rather than to changes in pupil performance' (Cooper and Good, 1983, p. 17).

We've tried dealing with this in a couple of ways. One approach is to give the pupil the information and ask them to take responsibility. Here, you explain the sustaining expectations effect in teaching. 'Your teachers are working with hundreds of pupils each week,' you can say. 'They might not notice a change in you for some time yet.' We go further: 'Your parents might not either. Other people – friends, peers, family – might hold on to a version of you that no longer exists, and only modify their perception of you a month or six weeks down the line. This will be a tough period during which you are the only person who can reward yourself, because you're the only person who knows this change is happening.' Finish the conversation by helping the pupil to set up a personal reward system that will sustain them through what might be a disappointing period.

Alternatively, you can talk to the teachers involved. Make it clear to them that you've explained to the pupil that teachers are busy and might not initially notice any change in levels of pupil effort or engagement. But ask them to notice soon – in the coming week or so. Often the pupil gets the boost in week two or three of the experiment, and it's a welcome one!

24. Effort Activity: The Effort Thermometer

If you want to be successful at anything you're going to have to put the work in – it's that simple.

There are a number of people who think that their talent is average, but their work ethic separates them from the rest. The actor Will Smith is a great example of someone who claims he doesn't have much talent and it's his work ethic that separates him from the rest. Here's what he says about hard work:

The only thing that I see that is distinctly different about me is I'm not afraid to die on a treadmill. I will not be out-worked, period. You might have more talent than me, you might be smarter than me, you might be sexier than me, you might be all of those things – you got it on me in nine categories. But if we get on the treadmill together, there's two things: you're getting off first or I'm going to die. It's really that simple, right?

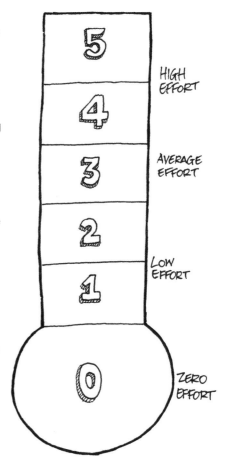

The effort thermometer is a way of getting you to keep track of how hard you're working. The first thing you have to decide is what are high levels of effort.

It might be best if you do this activity with your tutor group or ask a few friends for their thoughts. Next to 'high effort' write down what the high effort pupils are doing. (We've done this activity a number of times before. Here are the kinds of things we often get back: does ten hours of revision each week, always stays focused in class, works hard in every lesson, does additional work on top of homework, asks teachers questions to fix misunderstandings, attends lunchtime sessions or after-school catch-ups.)

Next, you then need to do the same for average effort and low effort pupils. How are the behaviours here different?

Now it's time to rate yourself. Be honest – no one else is ever going to see this. Where would you put yourself on the scale – low, average or high?

Once you've made your decision, answer the following questions:

1. Are you working hard enough yet?

2. Are you *reactive* (responding to teacher instruction only) or *proactive* (sorting things out yourself, setting yourself extra work, taking responsibility for your own progress)? Place a cross on the line below to represent where you think you might be:

Reactive   **Proactive**

Why have you made this decision? Make a note of the evidence:

_____

3. What things could you change? How could you push the cross further to the right?

4. Make a note of three or four pupils who are working harder than you. What are they doing?

5. Have you got the balance right between work and rest? What adjustments could you make?

Repeat this activity every term: as you progress through the year, the amount of effort you need to put in changes.

25. Effort Activity: Packing My Bags

Often, our perception of our own effort is inaccurate. We frequently judge it by the people we surround ourselves with. So, if someone asked you how hard you are working, you might think about your three closest friends, figure out how you're doing compared to them and then give an answer. This is fine if all your friends are really hard working. If not, you might be kidding yourself that you're doing enough work.

It can be useful to do a checklist to review how hard you are working and see if you need to make any changes.

Have a go. First, you need to look at the behaviours listed below and then decide is this something you do consistently (at least once every week), sometimes (at least every three weeks to a month) or rarely (once a term or even never). Then you have to decide whether you think this is a development need (something you should improve). If you think that it's something you should consider as a development need, your final task is to prioritise it as either high, medium or low, depending on how you think it will impact your performance.

Behaviour	Demonstrated consistently/ sometimes/rarely	Development need: high/medium/low
I always hand my homework in on time.		
I leave things until the last minute.		
I do the minimum amount of work I can get away with.		
I hand in extra exam work for marking.		
In most classes my main goal is to do the minimum needed so I don't have to work very hard.		
I work hard at home.		
I do ten hours a week of independent study at home.		

February

The next step is to decide what you are happy with and what you aren't happy with.

This activity uses the analogy of packing your bags for a holiday. Imagine you're leaving the present you behind and moving to a new you. There are going to be some things that you want to take with you – elements of your current habits and work practices that you really like – and some things that you will definitely want to leave behind – things that annoy you about yourself or end up causing you stress and anxiety.

Use the table below and decide what you need to improve (put those in the 'pack to take' column) and what you need to leave behind.

Pack to take	Leave behind

Finally, you need to decide on a date – that is, the date you're leaving behind all the stuff you don't want to be part of your school life (everything you've put in the right-hand column).

Give yourself a few days. You'll need to be mentally ready to count down to this date and look forward to it. A tip: we've found it's good to make it a Thursday or Friday. It'll be tiring being the new you. Start on a Monday and by Wednesday you'll be exhausted! We've found that pupils have more success when they give themselves a day or two of their new self before a weekend comes along to save them …

26. Effort Activity: Twenty-Five Minute Sprints

There's a very famous book by Italian entrepreneur and author Francesco Cirillo called *The Pomodoro Technique*. Pomodoro is Italian for tomato. (The tomato in question is one of those novelty kitchen timers, not a real one!) We'll come back to the tomato in a bit.

In his book, Cirillo argues that we can generate lots of energy and effort by working in short bursts, even on long tasks that we don't feel motivated to do. Think of all the tasks you've got to do that you just can't bear to begin – there might be revision notes, essays to write, jumbled notes to file away or a piece of coursework to start.

Choose one that's become a bit of a nightmare for you – that's hanging over your head and you just don't want to do. Make a note of it here:

_____

Step 1

Now for the tomato. By which we mean getting hold of either a kitchen timer (needless to say, it doesn't have to be shaped like anything in particular!) or the timer on your phone.

Find somewhere quiet. Arrange the things you need to begin. You're going to do a twenty-five minute sprint. It's important to tell yourself this: *twenty-five minutes – that's all.* You're allowed no distractions whatsoever in that twenty-five minutes. Don't worry. You can be back on social media in twenty-five minutes' time, checking updates and messages.

Now start the timer and go!

Step 2

Congratulations! You've got that nightmare task started. All of a sudden, this job is going to seem less frightening. You'll be able to come back to it.

Some suggestions for messing around with the Pomodoro Technique:

1. Try twenty-five minutes on, twenty-five minutes off, twenty-five minutes on. It takes one hour and fifteen minutes in total, and you can do it at a regular time each night after school.

2. Try twenty-five minutes on, five minutes off, twenty-five minutes on, five minutes off, twenty-five minutes on. It takes about one hour and thirty minutes, and is a useful technique for really attacking a difficult piece of work.

3. Try measuring tasks in sprints. How many will it take? This way, you'll develop a sense of how you work, and you can begin picking off scary tasks more quickly and easily.

4. Try using sprints to review work. Suddenly you'll find yourself ahead and on top of things. It's a great feeling!

27. Practice Activity: The Nine-Box Grid

Before you really begin to attack your revision, you need to be able to actively recast the information you need to learn. That means rewriting or reorganising your class notes into something you have built yourself – something you've processed and created. No passive reading and highlighting of notes here – just active, engaged rewriting!

You don't want to be spending too much of your time on this – we recommend about 50% – but it's a crucial step.

One way to do it that we've really enjoyed is the nine-box grid. (An A level physics pupil taught us this one. He ended up at Oxford so we know it works!) And here's the best bit: all you'll need is a sheet of A4 paper.

Place the paper in front of you – orient it landscape – and fold it into thirds, like this:

Then, with it folded, do it again the other way so that when you open up you've got nine squares:

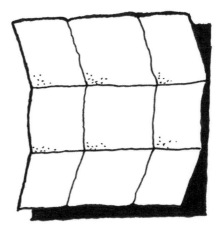

There are three steps to filling in the grid:

1. Your challenge is to summarise an entire topic (or, if you're feeling brave, an entire course) in nine boxes. First, you need to read through your notes on the topic/ course and decide what your nine boxes are. Ask yourself: what are the nine key subsections? Ask teachers to suggest nine. Work with friends to identify the nine. Go through exam papers to see if they help you decide on the nine.

2. Once you've got the nine subsections, you need to find a way to summarise your notes using just the little boxes on the grid. You can't use any additional space. Don't try to write so small you can't read it! Use diagrams, pictures, mind-maps or other graphic organisers to condense your information. Do what you have to, but get it all down in the nine little boxes. Then photograph it in case it gets lost!

3. Now read through the whole grid and, on the other side, draw up a list of key concepts, ideas and vocabulary you're going to need to master. That's it. An entire course or topic on one sheet of paper.

Once you've got your nine-box grid, you're ready to attempt exam questions. You'll see other pupils laboriously rereading their notes or copying out the entire course again in their lucky pen – but ignore them. You've got the content nailed on one sheet! You then need to move quickly on to testing your understanding, recall and ability to perform under exam conditions.

28. Practice Activity: Will vs. Skill

If you ask most pupils what they spend most of their revision time on, if they are honest they will say revising things that they like doing. It's quite normal when you think about it. We all like to spend time on activities we feel comfortable or confident doing.

The problem can be that we're putting off things we feel uncomfortable with or don't like doing.

Everyone has heard of Usain Bolt – the world's fastest ever 100 metre runner. He has an interesting way of approaching his training. He works out where his weak spots are and then spends most of his time training on them. For Bolt, that's the start of his 100 metres. He's a big guy and getting out of the blocks requires a lot of effort for him. He says he knows that it's his area of vulnerability. He's not great at it (he's 'low skill' when it comes to bursting from the blocks), and what's more, he doesn't particularly enjoy this aspect of his training (he is 'low will' in this area – that is, he has to force himself to do it, almost against his will). Despite these obstacles, Bolt spends a significant part of his training on this element because he knows that this is where he can improve the most.

The Will vs. Skill matrix is a useful way of helping you to identify where you need to spend your time practising. It's not just Bolt's idea; it was made popular in *The Tao of Coaching* by Max Landsberg. Let's see if it helps you like it helped Usain Bolt.

Step 1

Pick one of your subjects. Make a list of all the topic areas that you need to cover in your revision. If you've done a nine-box grid for the subject, this will be much easier.

Step 2

Next, put each of the topic areas into the grid below. You need to make two judgements about the topic area to place it correctly. First, how good at it are you (that's the level of skill)? Second, how keen on it are you (that's your level of will)?

» **High will/low skill.** Here you put the topics that you like doing but in which you are still developing your skills. For example, you might like research methods in sociology but you know that you need to develop your expertise.

» **High will/high skill.** Here list all the topics that you love doing and that you are good at.

» **Low will/low skill.** In this box write a list of the topics you don't like and in which you know that your skills need developing.

» **Low will/high skill.** This is an interesting box. It's for the topics you might not be keen on but which you are good at.

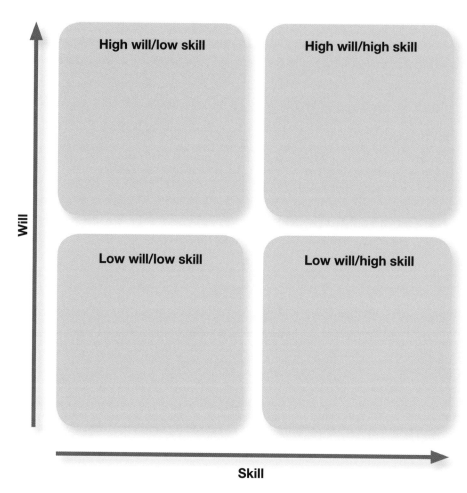

Source: Landsberg (2003), p. 55.

When you've added all the topics to the table, it's time for some reflection.

Where have you been spending most of your revision time? Is it time to tackle the low will/ low skill box?

Finally, when would be best to do this? Choose a high energy, positive time of day and line up a great reward for getting the job done!

9. March

Fight or Flight

February and March are the months, for us at least, where the wheels can come off. Where hastily constructed interventions are running furiously, pupils are going off the rails, after-school meetings with parents and agencies reach their peak and even our best pupils go through traumas that suggest they might not get the grades they deserve.

We've spent a lot of time over the last few years looking at how we might make pupils better at coping with these setbacks, tribulations and disasters – in short, at solving their own study problems. (There's a distinction to be made here: we're writing about socio-emotional problems – that is, ones with multiple possible solutions that are often in flux, rather than single solution problems grounded in subject knowledge, like a specific maths problem.) Having had hundreds of problem solving conversations with pupils over the years, one thing we've learned is that offering tailor-made solutions – tempting though it can be – only creates an acquired dependency where large numbers of pupils keep returning for more support. We've been guilty, looking back, at creating a cohort of anxious, needy learners who rely on us to get them through the day precisely because we would keep offering unsustainable solutions to get them through the day.

We knew we needed to make pupils better problem solvers, but for a long period we couldn't figure out how. A breakthrough of sorts came when we applied the principles, strategies and tools we were lucky enough to access through continuing professional development (CPD) and leadership training to our pupils. There are plenty of problem solving models and methods out there (you can research abstraction, hypothesis testing, means-end analysis, reduction and so on).

Our starting point was root cause analysis – the identification of the factors that cause or contribute towards the occurrence of an undesirable event. Our start was David Kolb's problem solving cycle (see McLeod, 2013) which encouraged us to examine a series of issues we wanted to solve – attendance, punctuality, levels of effort, culture and so on – by moving through four distinct stages of a problem solving and solution building cycle, rather than becoming mired in circular discussion and what some might call analysis paralysis. Kolb is a champion of 'experiential learning', so the cycle is designed to encourage iterations of problem, solution and reflection, encouraging us to spend an equal amount of time in each phase, and eschewing lingering in favoured phases or skipping sections of the process entirely, both of which we've seen before.

The tool is included in this chapter in its use-for-pupils form, but it's worth having a look at each phase here in order to explore what we learned and how best to use it. Kolb suggests a four-step cycle formed of simple questions that look like this:

1 What is currently happening?

2 Why is it happening this way?

3 What are your options?

4 How did it go, and what have we learned?

Pretty simple on the face of it, but beneath the surface are a host of interesting tenets and principles of problem solving that we've had success sharing with pupils.

What Is Currently Happening? Why Is It Happening This Way?

We've put these two together – counter-intuitive as it may seem – because they need to be kept apart (bear with us!). In these phases of the cycle, you're encouraging the pupil, or your team of staff, to draw up a list of verifiable facts and figures which describe current performance (what is currently happening?) and then a series of reasoned justifications that explain the current reality (why is it happening this way?).

Let's look at the first part of that sentence – a *list of verifiable facts and figures*. Watch out for the understandable tendency to use emotional adjectives in this phase. Pupils will tell you things are 'terrible' or 'rubbish', or worse, describe themselves as 'thick' or characterise a subject or issue as a 'nightmare' or 'disaster'. Your role will be to politely discourage this kind of contribution and look instead for objective reality. John Whitmore puts it nicely in his book, *Coaching for Performance* (2009, p. 71), where he suggests instead looking for 'facts and figures, incidents that occurred, the actions taken, the obstacles overcome, the resources and people available', avoiding value judgements and going for 'detailed, non-judgemental description'. Often, we've found that the pupil's emotional investment in the issue means they can't see clearly and find it hard to describe precisely what is happening. Consequently, they find this phase a real challenge.

We've read a lot about encouraging creativity in young learners and there are, perhaps unsurprisingly, a lot of commonalities between the creative process and the problem solving process. When describing a creative's behaviour in the early stages of idea development, texts often refer to the 'broadening of attention' needed to fuel potential ideas – a state of active seeing, a kind of deliberate and studied perception. (This relates to the dreamer stage of Robert Dilts' Disney Method – see below for more

on this.) You might need to send your pupil away on a fact-finding mission over a number of days to nail precisely what it is that's happening in a current subject. Likewise, when working with staff you might find you simply don't have the necessary information to adequately describe the problem (e.g. a sense that punctuality is poor without having any data), and that has to be your starting point.

Now the second half of the sentence: *a series of reasoned justifications that explain the current reality.* Two things to watch out for here. First, we've found a defensive tendency to rush from the what to the why, making it very difficult to keep the conversation on track. For example: 'I'm on a grade D in geography ...' (quick intake of breath) 'but that's because my teacher's been ill for the last three weeks and I lost my notes on the bus and once I had to sit next to X and I can't concentrate and the classroom's freezing and ...'

If you get this sort of response you can politely hold a hand up and return to the phase in question. ('Let's park the *why* for a moment. Can you return to telling me exactly *what* is happening, please?') We've found this happens with both pupils and staff, partly, we suspect, because the why is a more comfortable place – a list of often immutable woes that justify the current level of performance.

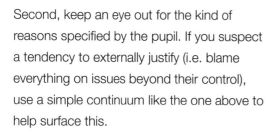

Internal justifications:

I guess I'm not really concentrating.

I haven't been keeping my notes up to date.

I don't get up early enough and miss the 8.05 bus.

I've lost the trust of my teacher.

I don't ask questions to clarify my understanding.

External justifications:

Everyone's noisy.

The topics are impossible.

The bus is always weirdly early.

Sir doesn't like me.

Maths is just so boring.

Second, keep an eye out for the kind of reasons specified by the pupil. If you suspect a tendency to externally justify (i.e. blame everything on issues beyond their control), use a simple continuum like the one above to help surface this.

Don't expect every reason to be an internal – and therefore solvable – justification. But if the vast majority (in some cases all of the reasons!) are externally justified, it's helpful to use the continuum to point it out. 'All the reasons you've listed are currently beyond your control,' you can say. 'Is there any way we can rephrase them to bring them across to the left of the continuum? By taking responsibility for them, you're much more likely to generate a solution.'

What Are Your Options?

Here's where the temptation to contribute is at its strongest. We've both been guilty in the past of jumping in at this point with our enthusiastically delivered 'ten things you've got to do to get this sorted'. It makes us feel useful, as though we're earning our money. And some of that support is going to be necessary, sure. But the focus of this section of the conversation needs to be on building the pupil's capacity to generate ideas. One way to do this is to reference and remember the classic Walt Disney approach, as modelled by Robert Dilts (1994). Disney used to take his creative staff through phases. In the dreamer phase, all ideas were considered entirely uncritically, distinct from any dull practicalities or operational issues. Just generate. It wasn't until the realist and critic phases that a more logical, rational approach would be encouraged, asking questions like, 'How are we going to get this done?' to test ideas generated in the dreamer phase.

We all have the tendency to sabotage ideas at the point of conception because we move immediately to realist practicality. To avoid this, ask pupils to set aside practical issues. 'Imagine there was some way of sorting that,' you can tell them. 'OK, back to generating ideas …'

Only add ideas of your own with permission. 'I think I might have a couple of options too. Do you want to hear them?' gives control to the pupil. One of the activities we've suggested in this chapter is The Action Priority Matrix (Activity 37), and that's a good one to use to frame this section of the conversation. You're looking for quick wins – that is, low effort, high impact strategies that have a good chance of giving an immediate sense of positive change. The aim is to generate as many possible ways forward rather than giving the sense that there is a 'correct' answer you're hoping they'll eventually alight upon.

How Did It Go? What Have We Learned?

The pupil becomes the experimenter now, and we move from theoretical discussion to practice.

The same levels of active attention are needed to accurately assess progress; a broadening and refining of perception. Encourage pupils to look for leading indicators of early success rather than choosing a longer term lagging indicator like, 'So after a few weeks, we should see your grades improve, right?' Consider qualitative outcomes, such as feeling better, concentrating harder, making more positive contributions in class, feeling more on top of study and just 'enjoying it more' as your early indicators of success. During the discussions of progress (or accounts of how nothing has changed!), adopt the demeanour of a researcher or scientist and model an engaged, enquiring, interested response to whatever happens.

If it hasn't worked, help the pupil return to the why, then refine and rebuild the plan. By modelling this process, you can go some way to giving control and responsibility to pupils, and require them to use the tool to attack other issues. If you're lucky, you'll create pupils who, rather than fly from problems, actively hunt them down!

29. Attitude Activity: The Problem Solving Cycle

This activity is based on the work of David Kolb of the University of Leicester. Kolb's work suggests that we learn best through experience – through doing. If we take action and attempt a challenge (therefore experiencing something rather than just reading or thinking about it) our awareness, understanding and mastery increases. Kolb proposes that 'experiential learning', as he calls it, passes through four phases.

When we first saw Kolb's work, his four phases were presented as a framework for problem solving. It worked really well for us and we became hooked. We'll share what we learned with you here. You'll need to set aside thirty minutes to start with.

First, choose a problem you're battling with or a barrier you're facing. It might be to do with study habits, current performance, levels of energy or a subject-specific issue.

The problem or barrier: _____

The result of the problem: _____

Now break down the problem into the four stages of Kolb's problem solving cycle. Use the guidance opposite to inform you how to approach each stage.

Each of us apparently has a preference for one of these stages and might have a tendency to linger in it or even stay there as long as possible. We all know someone who endlessly talks about a problem without ever doing something about it. That person might feel most comfortable in stage 2 – analysing the problem. Other people you know might leap to a swift conclusion and do something straight away without properly thinking it through – perhaps they feel less comfortable in stages 1 and 2 and want to hurry on to stages 3 and 4.

For the cycle to work, stay in each quadrant for a good period of time, getting the most out of each stage.

The solutions you come up with will be better ones as a result!

4. Experiment with a course of action

Key question: 'How did it go, and what have I learned?'

You'll be in this phase for a week. Try one of your top three adjustments. As you go along, get a sense of how it is working. Persist with it, thinking about its impact on your learning.

Then assess it at the end of the period. Discard, repeat or modify.

1. Explore the problem

Key question: 'What is currently happening?'

Stay here for ten minutes, assessing *the exact situation you are in.* Do not use judgemental or emotional language ('terrible', 'crap', 'nightmare'). Use facts and figures ('I'm on a grade E', 'My motivation is very low'). Dredge up every last bit of evidence you can find – grades, test scores, attendance, levels of effort and energy, feedback. Describe only – do not use 'because' yet; avoid justifying anything. Calmly list everything about your current situation.

3. Decide a course of action

Key question: 'What are my options?'

Stay here for ten minutes. Look back at what is happening and why. *Only focus on the things you can solve.* Calmly set aside things outside your control. Sift through your analysis of the problem and begin listing things you could do. Be uncritical; ignore the part of your brain saying, 'That's a terrible idea!' or 'How could that work? It's ridiculous!' and continue to list courses of action. Start with 'I could …' and go from there. When you're stuck, bring to mind everyone who could help – teachers, tutors, mentors, parents, family, friends.

When you've completed your list, choose your favourite three, then your top option.

2. Analyse the problem

Key question: 'Why is it happening?'

Stay here for ten minutes. List every single reason *why the problem is happening.* Make your list as long as possible, exploring yourself and your own actions, your attitudes and beliefs, the influence of those around you, your classrooms, lessons, work materials, the impact of external events, the impact of teachers and tutors and so on.

Calmly list everything, making sure nothing is missed. Do not bother yourself with solutions yet. Take your time.

30. Practice Activity: K-SPA

Chartered psychologist and university lecturer Alison Price is interested in the psychology of successful people. Having spent time researching and interviewing, she proposes an interesting model for the types of preparation people do before a breakthrough. These barrier busting breakthroughs don't come over night, Price argues – they're the result of careful planning, preparation and determined action.

But faced with a problem, it's normal to sometimes feel gloomy and defeated. It's really hard to know what great preparation should look like. How do we get past this? Where should we start? What should we do next?

We've had fun adapting Price's work to create the K-SPA model below. It suggests four things you should focus on in order to break through a barrier and become better at something. It's like a four-step plan to follow:

K = Knowledge. Things you need to *know more about* in order to break down the barrier.

S = Shopping. Things it would be *useful to have* to break down the barrier.

P = Practising. Things you *need to be better at* in order to break down the barrier.

A = Action. Things you could *do right now* to break down the barrier.

First, begin by identifying your barrier. You're capable of blasting it away in the next few weeks. Choose a barrier that is preventing you from improving; perhaps a problem you've identified using the previous activity (The Problem Solving Cycle).

The problem or barrier: _____

The result of the problem: _____

Now use the four headings to begin brainstorming solutions. Once you've got a whole bunch under each heading, your task is to choose the one that will have the highest impact, and commit to it. You should end up with four doable actions that you can now sequence!

Knowledge	Possible areas for research and learning:
	The one thing I'll study:
Shopping	Possible purchases:
	The one thing I'll buy:
Practising	Possible areas for practice:
	The one thing I'll practise:
Action	Possible actions I could take straight away:
	The one thing I'll do now:

The important thing here is to commit to the four actions. To maximise your chances of success, choose actions you know you can execute, and schedule them so you know when you should be taking that action.

If you're stuck or it didn't work, return to your list of possible actions and choose another!

31. Practice Activity: Spaced Practice

Studies show that snacking regularly on learning beats bingeing. In other words, rather than cram immediately before an exam, you can save time and energy by starting earlier and spacing out smaller sessions of practice and revision. You use your memory more this way. And as Benedict Carey says in his book *How We Learn* (2015, p. 40), 'using memory changes memory'. The more often something is recalled, the stronger the memory gets; a cycle of 'learn, forget, relearn, remember again' is strengthening your memory. A whole bunch of studies show that this process of spaced practice works way better than cramming. It also involves working for shorter periods rather than sitting down for epic sessions the night before an exam. That's a win-win.

But how do you space out practice? Well, that depends on how long it is before your exam. Since we're putting this activity in the March section of the book, we're going to build a programme of spaced practice that assumes three months until your exam, but if you're using this at another time of year, don't worry!

In a study undertaken at York University, researchers found that '… to achieve enduring retention, people must usually study information on multiple occasions'.* ('Enduring retention' is academic-speak for remembering information!) In other words – cramming is beaten by revisiting material a number of times – learning it, forgetting it and going back to re-learn it. Many studies have discovered that the spaces or gaps you leave within these study periods play a big part in how well you remember the material! If you've a test in a month, your gaps should be about a week – four tests, each a week apart. If it's three months – and we're assuming it is – your gaps need to be every two weeks.

So, for our purposes, you need to be reviewing topics every two weeks, allowing them to fade in the gaps, then refreshing them when the next test comes along.

* See Cepeda, N. J., Vul, E., Rohrer, D., Wixted, J. T. and Pashler, H. (2008). Spacing effects in learning: a temporal ridgeline of optimal retention. *Psychological Science* 19: 1095–1102.

You don't necessarily have to do this for all your exams. Start by choosing a subject that you think needs a boost and plan out some spaced practice using the grid below. We've given some examples to help get you started.

Week	1	2	3	4	5	6	7	8	9	10	11	12
Topic A	Revise		Deep review		Deep review		Deep review		Quick review		Quick review	
Topic B		Revise		Deep review		Deep review		Deep review		Quick review		Quick review
Topic C												
Topic D												
Topic E												
Topic F												

Note: Revise – an initial study of the topic, summarising it; deep review – an in-depth revision session, re-remembering everything; quick review – a shorter, light touch review, checking memory.

One more thing: look out for what researchers call the 'fluency illusion' – that is, the tendency for us to be able to recall facts very quickly immediately after study. It might make you think, 'I've got this nailed. I can do it!' That might not be the case. Let it fall into your subconscious during the gap, then try to recall it again.

32. Practice Activity: Test Yourself!

Dr Jennifer McGahan is a lecturer in psychology at Manchester Metropolitan University. Her research has focused on helping pupils to improve their memory, which is pretty useful for GCSE pupils. She shared this activity with us – many thanks, Jennifer. Over to you!

Taking a test does more than just assess your abilities; research has shown that it can also improve your memory for the information tested. Henry Roediger at Washington University has led the research in this area, now known as the 'testing effect'.

The term 'test' in this context refers to the act of retrieving information from your long-term memory. This can take many forms such as reciting facts about the Second World War aloud or completing a practice essay question. The test format is irrelevant; as long as you recall the information from memory, the rate at which you forget this information in the future is slowed down. This is in stark contrast to repeated study (reading over notes/highlighting text); when this technique is used information is forgotten much more quickly afterwards.

Despite huge amounts of research all showing the clear benefits of testing, most pupils prefer to revise for exams by reading information repeatedly. This is because the more you read something, the more familiar the content feels, resulting in a false sense of understanding and accomplishment. In contrast, testing yourself can feel challenging and frustrating, especially when you start to revise a new topic and it feels as though you are not recalling very much at all. Don't let this put you off: searching for the right answer (even unsuccessfully) strengthens the pathways in your brain for that information. Although it may feel counter-intuitive to test yourself, struggling is good for your brain and results in excellent learning in the end!

Remember that *all* exams require you to recall information; it is unlikely that an exam will test you on how well you can read text over and over again. Every time you test yourself you are reinforcing the connections in your brain in an outward direction, making them increasingly accessible for when you need it most – in an exam!

Top tips for testing yourself:

» Create elaborate links between new information and existing knowledge. This will make it easier to cue yourself during tests.

» Mind-maps are a great way of testing yourself. Close your books and scribble down everything you can remember. Number the points to track your progress.

» Feedback is essential when testing yourself to make sure that you do not learn any mistakes you may have made. This is especially important if you are using multiple choice tests as the right and wrong answers can be very similar.

How to Build a Killer Test

Step 1: Select a topic for study. Generate some headings and subheadings yourself that will act as cues.

Step 2: Close your books/switch off the computer and write down everything you can remember about your chosen topic. The first time you do this it may not be a lot of information, but stick with it.

Step 3: Review your work, check for any errors and correct these areas.

Step 4: Repeat steps 2 and 3 two more times.

Step 5: Change topic. Mixing up the topics tested results in greater memory recall.

Step 6: Two hours later try to recall the information selected in steps 2 and 5.

Step 7: One day later try to recall the information selected in steps 2 and 5.

33. Vision Activity: What's Stopping You?

This thing in front of you. This issue. This obstacle – this frustrating, unfortunate, problematic, unexpected problem preventing you from doing what you want to do … What if it wasn't so bad? Holiday (2015), p. 1

Deciding what your goals are and making a plan can, quite often, be the easy bit. We usually set off with good intentions and then *boom*, we get hit with an obstacle or a number of obstacles that slow us down or in some cases stop us from following through on our goals. The first thing to remember is that this is completely normal. As Ryan Holiday says in the quote above, if you have a goal worth pursuing it's likely that there are going to be some obstacles on the route. So don't beat yourself up about it. Accept this as part of the journey and plan a way through – it might not be that bad!

Sometimes these obstacles can be completely out of our control – a sudden change of circumstances in our life such as illness or family problems, for example. However, we sometimes think that these obstacles are out of our control when in fact we might be able to do something about them. This activity is one to do if you find that you're not making the progress you hoped for. There are four steps and you'll probably need to spend about five minutes on each stage.

Step 1: Remind Yourself What the Goal Is

My goal is …

I know I will have achieved the goal when …

I should have the goal completed by …

Step 2: Circles of Control

For step 2 you need some sticky notes. Write down all the obstacles you can think of on separate notes, one for each obstacle. Just keep writing and think of as many obstacles as you can. The next step is to place them on the circles of control diagram below. This is how it works. Take each sticky note and first ask yourself, how much control do I have over this? Is it no control – there is nothing you can do about it (e.g. external factors such as ill health or family problems)? Or could you influence the obstacle – it might appear out of your control but there are some things that you could do to make it better? Finally, is this something that is in your control (e.g. you might not have been working hard enough but you know there aren't really any excuses for this)?

Circles of control

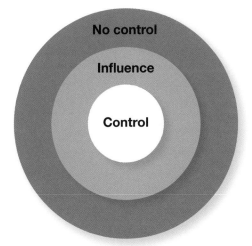

Source: Covey (1989), p. 82.

When you've decided where to place your sticky notes, it's sometimes useful to share your thoughts with another person, if you feel comfortable doing so. Sometimes we can believe we have no control when in fact we do. Getting a different perspective can sometimes help with this.

Step 3: Rate Your Obstacles

Next, take the sticky notes that you can influence or control and place them in the boxes below. You need to rate each obstacle on a continuum from 'stops me a bit' to 'stops me a lot' – think of it as a 1–10 scale.

If all of your notes are out of your control, you will need to seek some external support. Arrange to see your tutor or a mentor and describe the task you've done.

March

Stops me a bit   **Stops me a lot**

Step 4: The Action Plan

Now it's time to take action. Take the three sticky notes that appear to be stopping you the most and place them in the boxes below. You then need to answer the three questions on each obstacle and decide what action you're going to take.

Obstacle	What could I do to overcome this obstacle?	What options haven't I considered?	What actions can I take?

10. April

Changing Lanes, Finding Flow

Rarely is a holiday approached with such a gathering sense of dread as the Easter break when we've got Year 11 classes. We know those seventeen days are a priceless opportunity to break the back of exam preparation. We may be super-upbeat on our return ('If you had a disaster over the holidays and didn't get anything significant done, don't worry. We can still turn it around from here!'), but deep down we know that if Easter goes badly, there's a mountain to climb. We invest huge amounts of time on pre-Easter preparations, and many of the tools we've developed are included in this chapter.

Self-regulation can be taught – a better approach, we reckon, than the tendency to micromanage the pupil experience over the Easter holidays (school stays open, extra classes are put on, kids are tempted in by cake and fellowship, content is crammed again and we create dependent learners ill-equipped for Key Stage 5 and beyond).

If you're interested in using March and early April to explore self-regulation, a good place to start is by introducing flow theory. Most people are pretty familiar with the notion of 'flow states', but for those who aren't here's a potted history. Mihaly (pronounced Me-High) Csikszentmihalyi (Chicksent-Me-High) first coined the term 'flow' in the 1960s, using it to describe a similar state of fully engaged, fluid and trance-like work. In an interview with John Geirland in 1996, Csikszentmihalyi describes a feeling of complete immersion in an activity: 'The ego falls away. Time flies. ... Your whole being is involved, and you're using your skills to the utmost.' The chances are we've all felt it, perhaps while running, painting, playing a game or writing. A vast number of interviews with dancers, musicians, rock climbers, artists, surgeons, chess players and people from all disciplines and cultures convinced Csikszentmihalyi of the existence of flow states. Later in his career he turned his attention to the factors that contribute to the creation of flow states, concluding that they commonly arrive during the execution of 'painful, risky, difficult activities that stretched the person's capacity and involved an element of novelty and discovery' (Csikszentmihalyi, 1997, p. 110).

Csikszentmihalyi went on to suggest the core components that demarcate a flow state. There are ten. For the sake of simplicity and practicality the four we use are:

1 Clear goals, expectations and rules: awareness of what makes good performance, what the aims are, what will be judged (obtained from mark schemes, examiners' reports and examples of pupil work).

2 High levels of concentration and absorption: we've explored environment as a contributor to this.

3 Immediate feedback: not necessarily from a teacher or mark scheme. Think qualitative feedback, a sense of whether things are going well or need adjustment.

4 Balance between ability level and challenge: the task is challenging but 'appropriately aligned with one's skill set and abilities' (Kotler, 2014, p. 30), which gives some sense of control over the situation, even if it's not complete and confident.

It was the final point that we found the most challenging and interesting. If we were to encourage pupils to aim for flow states during exam preparation, we'd need to help them strike this balance as they worked; to find the sweet spot where challenge and ability level meet. Luckily, we had the flow states chart to help us. First proposed by Csikszentmihalyi in 1997, the chart works as a sort of map (see Figure 10.1).

It attempts to describe the emotional state a learner finds themselves in depending on a task's level of challenge versus the learner's level of skill. When a teacher designs a lesson, the pupil is moved around the map by a series of differentiated tasks which push them out of their zone of comfort towards

Figure 10.1. The flow model

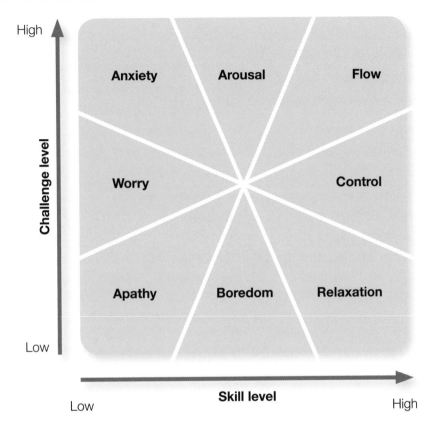

Source: Adapted from Csikszentmihalyi (1997).

the bottom of the map and nudge them from one region to another. The pupil isn't necessarily in control here (though there may be an element of adjustment they can make), the teacher is.

What's interesting is seeing what kind of curriculum the pupils design for themselves when working independently. Ask a learner to describe how they feel when they revise for German, English literature or history, and listen

for a response that, however it is expressed, may be aligned with one of the states on Csikszentmihalyi's chart. Apathetic or bored learners feel that way because, for example, they have designed a learning experience with insufficient challenge. Stressed learners might be working on material that is currently beyond their capabilities.

It's a fascinating chart, one we've studied and shared with pupils for years, but, if we're honest, we've struggled to make work. Despite numerous presentations in which we explore flow and give pupils advice about how best to reach flow states, we've felt a lack of concrete advice about precisely how to maximise your chances of experiencing flow.

Recently, we feel we've got closer. We've recast the diagram using a metaphor inspired by Csikszentmihalyi himself – water. We've found the mental model of the swimming pool to be one most pupils can get their minds around (Figure 10.2). Notice the change from *arousal* (apt to cause sniggers!) to *potential*.

Here's why the metaphor works for us, and the language we use to discuss and explain it.

Lane 1, where the water is warm and shallow, is where progress is comfortable and slow. As the depth of the water suggests, learning is confined to memorising surface features of material, reviewing simple content or working on areas that are already strengths. The warm temperature suggests comfort and ease. Here's where gentle work often becomes play; where we might end up splashing about and chatting. We swim slowly, or even wade, through apathy and boredom to relaxation, where we often stay.

Figure 10.2. Swimming pool model

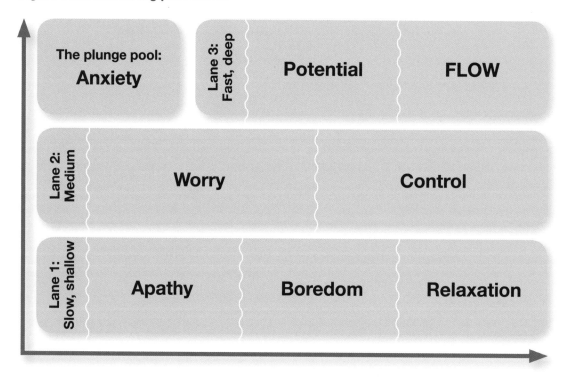

To ever reach lane 2, you need to struggle, by raising and sustaining a new level of challenge. Lane 2 is cooler and the swimmers move faster. The water is deeper too; there's no wading here – learning is harder, material is examined more deeply, questions are asked, weaknesses are focused on. The movement from lane 1 to lane 2 isn't pleasant. We feel the change in temperature and wince as we lower ourselves in. There's tension and anxiety as we assess the speed that others are going. Increased depth and challenge means increased learning speed … eventually. But to begin with, we might feel we're thrashing about a little, feeling exhausted, and that's normal. The struggle that precedes flow is a recognised part of the cycle. Soon, we're acclimatised and beginning to feel good. Lane 1 feels weirdly uncomfortable once we've done an extended spell in lane 2.

We might not reach lane 3 in one session. Many swimmers might take a break, internalise the struggle of lane 2 and recover before taking the next challenge. Lane 3 is cool and deep, and the step-up is immediately noticeable. Swimmers move quickly, cutting through the water. Again, we might feel a prickle of anxiety or fear as we slip into the pool and contemplate the challenge ahead, but lane 2 has taught us to maintain a feeling of control even when faced with difficulties. As we begin to move through the deep water (i.e. handle challenging work, review weaknesses,

tackle the hardest questions we can find), we may feel a sense of potential; that we're close to something we can't reach. Eventually, we hit flow; time means nothing and we work, gliding quickly, adjusting our technique in response to internal qualitative or external quantitative feedback as we go.

Sometimes we take a wrong turn, lose our way a little and wind up in the plunge pool – a place of anxiety, almost panic. It's freezing cold in there; churning like an icy hot tub. We take a dip in the plunge pool because we've misjudged the movement from lane to lane, taken on something too challenging and lost our sense of direction. It's a nasty experience, and so some swimmers stay in lane permanently, aware that they could be making more progress but content to reassure themselves that at least they've avoided an uncomfortable dunking. The good thing about the plunge pool is that once you're out, every lane feels warmer.

What Lane Are You In?

By adding these broad horizontal strokes to the diagram and thinking in terms of lanes, we've found that pupils can better assess where they are, and therefore make better judgements about the effectiveness of their personal independent learning curriculum.

In a coaching situation, there are questions that help do this:

» How comfortable does it feel where you are? (Often, though not always, we've found strong connections between lane 1 and physical as well as mental comfort. Follow-up questions about precisely where a pupil is when they work can yield locations like: lying on the sofa, on my bed, under a blanket, in an easy chair. We've found, on the whole, notions of physical comfort vanish as learners approach flow. A spartan chair and table are all that's required.)

» How warm/shallow does it feel where you are? What's the most difficult thing you've done in a recent revision session?

» What level of worry do you feel where you are? How regularly are you failing at a challenge you've set or hitting obstacles when you work?

» Do you ever feel as though time flies when you revise? Do you find yourself immersed in a problem or question?

Giving pupils the opportunity and tools for assessing the lane they spend most time operating in equips them to self-regulate over the two-week Easter break. For some, at least, it might encourage a critical assessment of the temperature and depth of their water, and a subsequent raising of challenge. Without the information about flow, pupils often lack the awareness to change the way they're working.

Changing Lanes: The Importance of Worry

Changing lanes means upping the level of challenge. The beginning of lane 2 is labelled worry, and the beginning of lane 3 is up close to the anxiety plunge pool. This is something it pays to point out to learners. Make sure to avoid a generalised statement such as 'worry is good'; we've learned that since pupils often worry about the wrong things, such a statement can be falsely comforting. By worry, we mean an uncomfortable sense that you can't successfully complete the challenge you've just set yourself; in other words, a task-specific worry of potential failure that might be expressed in a thought like, 'I'm *really* not sure I can pull this off.' This kind of worry is good – a sign that you've changed lanes. This is the feeling, we often tell pupils, that we should be chasing.

Of course, learners need to be equipped with the resources to be able to up their level of challenge. If you've given them exam questions differentiated into three broad lanes, for example, you've done a good job. Watch out for comfortable lane 1 swimmers who 'lose' harder questions or 'can't download' the handy resource you've prepared. Fixed mindset pupils rarely experience flow because the journey to it requires struggle, risk, setback and failure – all things they feel will confirm their intrinsic belief in their fixed ability.

34. Practice Activity: Finding Flow

Many social scientists and academic researchers have become interested in the idea of 'flow'.

Flow is a high concentration, high performance state that we can all experience when we have the right task in front of us, the right space around us and the right balance of challenge and skill. You might well have reached what researchers call a 'flow state' before:

» If you've ever become so absorbed in a task that time seems to fly – perhaps writing, painting or playing sport.

» If you've ever sat down to work on something (it might not be schoolwork, maybe a personal project) and hours seem to have gone by in the blink of an eye.

» If you've been so focused that a two-hour exam might feel as though it's gone by in half an hour.

» If you've ever suddenly felt as though you're totally 'in the zone'. A sort of fully engaged, complete concentration on something fascinating and difficult.

People seem capable of amazing work when they're in flow. They make swifter progress, they learn quickly, they stretch and challenge themselves, and they operate at a higher level. They seem to expend more mental effort and often feel pretty exhausted afterwards.

Lots of social scientists have studied and written about how to reach flow states. Two observations have emerged:

1. There seems to be a connection between *flow* and *challenge*. You can't reach flow doing something so easy it doesn't require your full concentration.

2. There's a connection between *flow* and *your level of skill*. You can't reach flow trying to attempt something that's way beyond your current capabilities.

But get the right balance of challenge and skill, and you begin to approach flow. One social scientist has produced a kind of emotional map to show us where flow is. We've reproduced a version of it here.

Think of a swimming pool with three lanes like this:

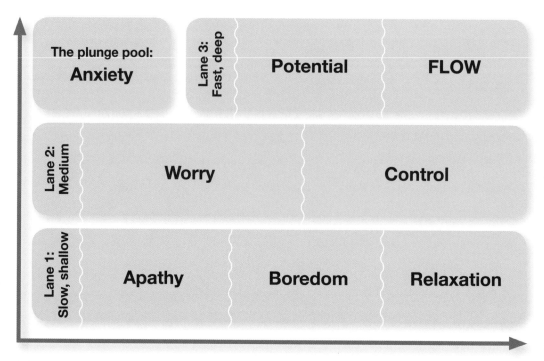

In lane 1 the water is warm. In other words, it's a nice, safe and comfortable place to be. The tasks here are low challenge and the work is easy. Even as your skill level increases, if you're in lane 1 you always feel relaxed.

In lane 2 the water is deeper and colder. It feels uncomfortable getting in if you're used to the warm water of lane 1. Swimmers move faster here – in other words, the work is harder. It often feels worrying, but stay long enough and you begin to feel in control.

In lane 3 the water is deep and cold. It's hard work here until you get used to it. Tasks are challenging and swimmers cut through the water quickly. Flow occurs in lane 3. There's no other way to get to it than by moving from lane 1, through lane 2 to lane 3.

The plunge pool – argh! Sometimes you try to move lanes too quickly, and end up losing your way and finding yourself in the plunge pool of anxiety. It's freezing in there! If you ever feel panic, if you feel overwhelmed or fearful, step back a little. Find a warmer, safer lane. Build your confidence there and then try to swap lanes again.

What Lane Are You In?

It could be that you're in different lanes for different subjects. So let's review your revision in just one subject.

Subject: _____

How do you feel when you revise for this subject? Return to a memory from the last revision session you did. Now check that memory against the three lanes of the flow swimming pool. Your word might not be one of the words in the pool, but is it similar to one of them? Which lane do you think you're in at the moment?

Changing Lanes

Changing lanes is about increasing challenge. If you're interested in changing lanes, remember:

» You need to choose harder revision tasks to up your level of challenge and change lanes.

» This will start by feeling uncomfortable. Worry, stress or anxiety might be the emotions you begin to feel at first.

» But these feelings will disappear the longer you stay. Control or potential might be the states that replace it.

Let's finish by making a list of revision activities you could be doing. If they're easy and comfortable put them in lane 1. If they make you feel uncomfortable or slightly worried put them in lane 2. If the thought of them makes you feel dread and fear put them in lane 3.

Lane	Indicative emotions	Activity
1	Comfort, ease, confidence, boredom	
2	Worry, discomfort, uncertainty	
3	Dread, fear, stress	

Next time you're feeling that progress is slow and you're comfortable and bored, you know it's time to change lanes. Choose an activity from a deeper, colder lane of the pool!

35. Practice Activity: High Flow Spaces

The places we choose to work in often have a big impact on how effective our work is. Our environments can influence the quality of our concentration and focus in both positive and negative ways. An interesting study by two researchers at Reading University, Derek Clements-Croome and Li Baizhan (2000), found that UK office workers felt significantly less productive as their work environment became more crowded or cramped, as temperatures varied or as the quality of light diminished. A large majority of the subjects interviewed estimated they might get a 10% rise in productivity if their environment was better.

We've seen similar effects with thousands of pupils over twenty years of teaching. And, surprisingly, we've seen pupils who deliberately sit down to work in noisy, distracting locations so they can be disturbed. When we meet to talk about their lack of progress, they'll often tell us, 'Well, I tried to work, but I couldn't concentrate,' or 'I like working with lots of people around me.' Inevitably, when we check the quality of their work, they've expended lots of time but in fact got very little done.

What are your work environments like, and what link might they have to your levels of focus, concentration and flow? By figuring out where you work best, you can increase your levels of concentration – and get more quality work done in less time.

School Spaces

Try walking your school or college environment and mapping where your high concentration, high flow spaces might be. Visit study rooms, workspaces, your library and so on. Look out for:

» The levels of foreground and background noise in these rooms.

» The number of other people there.

» The behaviour of the other people there.

» The quality of the seating spaces (the tables, chairs and desks).

» The levels of light.

More than anything, try to capture a feeling – is this place calm and focused? If it is, you will be too.

Then make a list of places to go when you really need to get a job done – your high flow spaces – and places to avoid, even when the worst part of yourself might be persuading you to go there!

High flow spaces:	Positive qualities:
Low flow spaces:	**Negative qualities:**

Home Spaces

Now have a look at the space you have at home. It might be a shared space or a space you have to yourself. Try to examine it with fresh eyes. What is your desk like? What about the space around you? Is there a corner of your room which is a calm, quiet, high flow space?

If not, you need to make one. If you can't, you need to find a surrogate study space that is neither school nor home – an in-between space.

In-between Spaces

Think about your wider environment – the public spaces between school and home. Many pupils we've worked with over the years have found the perfect coffee shop or local library in which to revise or do independent work or prepare for tests. Other have worked on long bus or train journeys.

Draw up a list of places to investigate. Make sure they're easy to get to so that you can incorporate them into a new routine.

Changing Spaces

Benedict Carey, in his book *How We Learn*, discusses some fascinating research about environment and memory. Research shows that changing the space in which you study increases your chance of remembering the material you've studied. Something about the freshness and variation in space makes the material more easily accessible in your memory. Swap high flow study spaces often and you may well remember more of what you've studied. So, the more high flow study spaces you have at your disposal, the better you'll do!

36. Vision Activity: Now vs. Most

There's a famous quote, sometimes attributed to US president Abraham Lincoln, that goes like this: 'Discipline is choosing between what you want now, and what you want most.' It's a useful idea to think about because in many circumstances what we want now (to buy a pair of trainers, say) probably damages what we want most (to have enough money to go on holiday).

Many of us will find ourselves choosing what we want now over what we want most; it's human to sometimes make these choices. In fact, in some circumstances the 'now' choice (taking a break and forgetting our troubles for an evening) doesn't really damage the 'most' goal (getting great GCSE grades), so it's OK if we choose it. The problem comes if we *continually* prioritise 'now' over 'most' – if we do, we never end up reaching the goal we've set ourselves.

This exercise is an opportunity to look at the temptations you face now, to analyse how damaging they might be and to take stock of how often you choose them. It can help you to keep a check on your tendency to prioritise 'now' over 'most', not by denying yourself everything you want but by reaching a healthy balance.

Step 1

Begin in the right-hand column of the table below. Make a note here of *what you want most* out of your final GCSE year. It should include the grades you would be delighted to get but also the consequences of those grades: the pride and happiness others will feel, your sense of success and confidence, the courses you can go on to study as a result, the school or college you hope to attend, the friends you hope to be with and the personal qualities you want to have developed by the time you finish your courses.

Step 2

Now the left-hand column. Here, list everything you're tempted by on a daily basis: to skip homework, binge watch TV, avoid revision, spend time on social media – anything that pulls you away from your long-term goals on a daily or weekly basis.

What you want now	What you want most

Step 3

Now we're going to make a check of which 'now' activities are the most damaging. For each 'now' activity, give it two scores:

1. Give it a *regularity score*: 0 = you almost never do it, 1 = you sometimes do it, 2 = you often do it, 3 = you pretty much always end up doing it.

2. Give it a *damage score*: 0 = it does almost no damage to what you want most, 1 = it does a small amount of damage to what you want most, 2 = it does some damage to what you want most, 3 = it does a lot of damage to what you want most.

Now, times the two numbers together for each 'now' activity. Once you've done that, every activity in that column should have a score between 0 and 9.

Activities that score 4 or more present a challenge for you. You do them reasonably regularly and they have a negative effect. These are the ones you need to take a longer look at.

If your list is huge, don't worry – that's pretty normal. *Choose one or two as your priorities.* If you can begin by making a change to just one or two behaviours, you can work from there. If you feel your motivation dip, return to your lists and look at the right-hand column – remind yourself of what it is you really want.

37. Systems Activity: The Action Priority Matrix

As you move through the exam season, time will be limited and the pressure will be on. Inevitably, there are going to be moments when you have too much to do and not enough time to do it in. Here's where an action priority matrix can be super-useful. It's a real lifesaver because it allows you to differentiate between tasks according to how much impact they are going to have on your learning relative to the amount of energy you'll need to get them finished.

The grid looks like this:

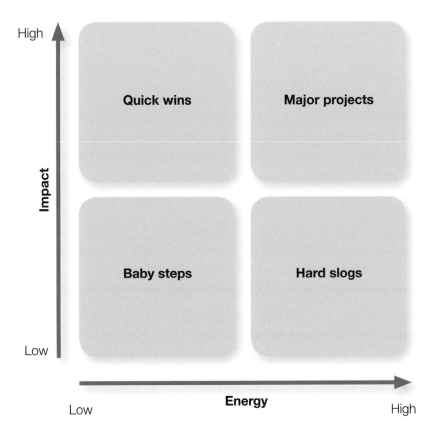

If you've got too much to do, try plotting all your possible actions on this grid. List everything you could be doing to prepare for the next two or three exams. Now weight them. First, consider how much energy they'll require. Energy means high concentration, focused time. If it's lots, put the action towards the right. If you could do it quickly and easily, put the action towards the left.

Second, consider the potential impact on your learning. If it's high – if you feel the action could really transform your knowledge or skills – put it up towards the top. If you think it will improve your learning a little, put it towards the bottom.

Once you've got all your possible options on the grid, have a look at which of the four quadrants the actions have fallen into and check out the advice below.

Quick Wins

These are gold. Get them done as a matter of urgency! They won't take long, and they could well transform your performance in a particular subject. If you've got an afternoon ahead of you (maybe even a full day, lucky you!), get these tasks done while you're feeling fresh and lively. Set a time limit for them – say to yourself, 'I'll do this task in thirty minutes' or 'I'll give myself an hour to get this finished.' Don't consider any other activities on the grid until you've bust through all of these.

Baby Steps

These tasks won't take much effort but neither will they have a massive impact. However, they could be good tasks to do if you're feeling foggy or lacking energy. They might not require total concentration, so if you need something to do just to get you into the rhythm of working, choose one or two. Similarly, if you've got a spare half an hour before lunch, or a spare twenty minutes before your bus, you could fire off one of these. Try doing one on the way into school for an exam – on a bus or train or in an environment that's not great for total concentration.

Major Projects

These are going to really boost your understanding and skill in a particular subject, but they're going to take a long period of high concentration to complete. Choose them if you can fulfil the following criteria:

» You have two to three hours where you won't be interrupted.

» You're committed to switching off all mobile devices for two to three hours, and you won't allow yourself to check them again, no matter what.

» You have access to a reasonably calm and quiet working environment.

If you can't fulfil these criteria, either change things so you can (call and cancel a meet-up, pull out of another commitment or switch location) or break the activities up. We've seen pupils have real success by taking a sledgehammer to a big project and bashing it into five or six smaller pieces. So instead of 'reread the complete chemistry textbook' (definitely a 'major project'!), pupils have broken the task down into 'reread chapter 1 and make notes' or 'reread sections 4 and 5, picking out key ideas'. Suddenly, the big project becomes a set of smaller tasks that might end up in 'quick win' or 'baby steps'.

Hard Slogs

If you're really pushed for time, the chances are you'll end up not doing these; all your energies should be spent on getting your quick wins done, building up a load of activities in baby steps or breaking your big projects down into more manageable tasks.

Watch out, though – sometimes we might put an activity into 'hard slog' because we just don't want to do it. Could it be that you've subconsciously underestimated the impact the task could have on your learning? Only keep the task in 'hard slogs' if you're super-sure.

It's worth using this grid throughout May and June just to check in with yourself, to work out what you could be doing and to pick off those tasks which will have the highest impact.

38. Attitude Activity: Benefit Finding, aka The Rocky Road

Two psychologists, Robert Emmons and Michael McCullough (2003) at the University of Miami, asked this question: what if we reviewed stressful and difficult times and turned our attention to the lessons we learned from those negative experiences?

Three hundred pupils were asked to reflect on challenging periods of their lives: poor results, breaking up with partners, feeling insulted or offended, or being rejected from a particular course. Of the 300 subjects, 100 were asked to specifically focus on the lessons they had learned – the positive benefits that had eventually come from these challenges. It turned out that it was these pupils who coped better with their disasters and moved on from them. Emmons and McCullough found that positive benefits could flow from negative experiences.

David Collins, professor of coaching and performance at the University of Central Lancashire, has coached at the very top level, including being responsible for UK athletics at the Beijing Olympic Games. Collins, with his colleague Áine MacNamara, has done similar work to Emmons and McCullough. He's discovered that top athletes have travelled what he calls a 'rocky road'. This means that they've usually had their fair share of setbacks, failures and disappointments along the way. Often, we don't get to hear about these setbacks – we only hear about the successes!

The rocky road

SUCCESS

What people think it looks like

SUCCESS

What it really looks like

Professor Collins suggests that the rocky road might even be good for you as you will develop some useful skills along the way. The key thing is not to dwell on the setback and to bounce back.

Your exam period is going to bring challenges and difficulties, but you can use them as fuel. Think about a recent negative experience and look at the ten suggestions below. You don't have to address all of them but aim to make notes under at least five.

1. A personal quality that has strengthened because of the experience.

2. A personal quality you didn't have at all that you've now begun to develop.

3. An increased appreciation of some part of your life as a result of the experience.

4. A valuable lesson you've extracted from the experience.

5. A realisation about life that you might not have ever considered before the experience.

6. An increased confidence about the way the world, or certain people, work because of what happened to you.

7. A skill you've developed or consolidated (e.g. thinking through problems, reflecting and understanding, communicating ideas, arguing confidently) because of the experience.

8. A relationship that has strengthened, perhaps with someone who helped or supported you through the experience or a stronger relationship with someone who hurt you.

9. A 'rule' you have extracted from the experience that you can now test in new situations.

10. A reassessment of certain priorities that might have happened because of the experience.

The piece of writing you've done will remind you that we grow as a result of difficult times. Keep it somewhere close and refer to it when you need to!

11. May

Well-Being and Stress Management

As the exam season approaches, even the best prepared can have moments of personal crisis. For the less fortunate, May is slow-motion trauma. There are a plethora of agencies who can help your pupils with genuine mental illness; the following is designed to help the fortunate majority.

We've found there's been a pretty significant gap between researching the principles of mind management and implementing anything effective. Like many schools, our first forays into encouraging positive self-regulation and stress management strategies were through running drop-in sessions that nobody attended and then, fired-up and frustrated, leading en masse activities delivered to an entire disengaged year group. Neither, in our case, were particularly effective (we're sure many of you will have had considerably more success).

We've since used one-to-one coaching conversations or smaller intervention sessions (of around six to eight pupils) to introduce and discuss the management of anxiety and stress. Even then, there's been a sense that pupils are aware of the information – try to find a Year 11 pupil who doesn't know they should be getting eight hours of sleep a night – but that, for whatever reason, they aren't acting on it or applying it in their own lives. There's an additional complication: we've found that three consecutive days of practice are often needed before there is any sense of things improving. That's why the bulk of the activities included here attempt to be as practical as possible; a set of instructions from which the pupils cannot deviate and a time frame within which they must persist. The mantra is that staying positive involves engaging in solution focused behaviour, rather than repeating damaging routines and habits.

Before the activities, though, there are a set of shorter, smaller suggestions and observations drawn from a variety of sources – a sort of grab-bag of advice that we've been developing and using ad hoc over the period in which we've developed the VESPA system but which aren't appropriate for an entire activity.

Going Dark and Sleep

The blue-green light of late night screen use, as we probably all know, encourages melatonin production in the brain, and 'tricks' us into thinking it's daytime. Sleep becomes elusive, levels of concentration drop and the ability to control difficult or damaging emotions falls away pretty steeply. We've done a whole raft of assemblies on going dark, digital detoxing and championing

the importance of airplane settings (with examples of pupils who've done it). We've worked with gamers to arrange a pre-exam deletion of apps and games, with a calendared date at which they can be re-uploaded. We've gone through signing off messages on social media feeds ('Back in a month!' type stuff) and so on. Many of the above have been really effective.

A telling question has been, 'What do you use as an alarm clock?' The answer, invariably nowadays, is 'my phone'. Encourage pupils, or parents if you can get hold of them, to invest in a cheap analogue alarm clock so that pupils can leave their phones on charge downstairs at the end of the day. Screen time within an hour of bedtime can disrupt sleep patterns (most kids know this) so we've worked to timetable TV schedules with habitual late night TV watchers. Often, habit change is promoted by the use of a surrogate – audiobooks or reading to replace TV, for example. Make the new habit as fail proof as possible by choosing stories that are hardwired for feelings of comfort and happiness. Old favourites from Year 8 or 9 might help (Louis Sachar's *Holes*, anyone?).

The emphasis must be on solution focused behaviour, as we've mentioned. It's worth pointing out that without a commitment to change, the pupil will continue to feel frazzled, stressed and out of control.

Caffeine, Protein and Sleep

It's helpful to raise awareness about caffeine levels in energy drinks and soft drinks; pupils are pretty clued up on sugar content but we've come across a significant number who think Diet Coke is free from everything and therefore a safe bet for continual consumption. There are a whole host of online resources continually updated about caffeine in soft drinks, giving you milligrams per 100ml of liquid (watch out for US sites where drinks have higher levels). In the UK, Diet Coke comes in at about 12mg, as does Lucozade; Pepsi at around 10mg. Red Bull and Rockstar are up in the early 30s – that's about half a cup of coffee's worth.

Protein-rich foods give an energy boost before bed where carbs promote drowsiness. We've found super-healthy gym types know their low-carb diet pretty well but make the mistake of hoovering up protein-heavy suppers which prevent good sleep. Late eating and drinking generally doesn't help; no caffeine after 4pm seems a pretty standard rule of thumb (though for us, it seems to be earlier – 1 or 2pm).

Again, it's a case of monitoring current behaviour, finding patterns and – the solution focused bit – committing to small adjustments and trying your best to make them happen.

Exercise

For runners, swimmers and gym-goers this is an easy one. For the rest of us, there's always walking.

We've experimented with helping learners with walking for mindfulness or therapy in the past. One of our walking activities, There and Back, is in *The A Level Mindset*, and has been used by Birmingham University's Character Education project. If you're interested in exploring it, ask your pupils to block out an hour of their time and ensure they'll be alone and undisturbed.

They need to:

» Choose a destination that is about a twenty minute walk away.

» Walk there. Tell them that while they walk they can only think positive thoughts. The topic is: things I am good at, things I am thankful for. Nothing else can enter their mind. If they find their concentration wandering, they should gently bring it back and keep focusing on these two topics. When they arrive, or as they go, ask them to record their thoughts or list them quickly on a notepad.

» Then the pupil returns to where they set out. While they walk back, they're allowed to address their problems. But here's the thing – the topic is: things I can do to solve my problems. Again, the key is to be strong with themselves. This is the only thing they can think of, and if their thoughts deviate they should bring them back as soon as they realise what's happened. When they arrive back, encourage them to take a few minutes alone and make a note of their thoughts and ideas.

Some people repeat this activity a couple of times a month to help them refocus. One person we know has the top of a hill as their destination – they say that walking down it helps to relax them after the hard slog of getting to the top, and they always come up with actions they can take to solve problems on the way down.

There's also mindful walking to consider. We've read a whole host of advice on this and distilled it into our version, in which pupils take a short, daily walk during May and June – it can be as little as ten minutes. Choosing a circuit that takes about that long to walk is part of the discussion and preparation. Their aim is to focus, while they walk, on (1) the quality of their breath – they can use box breathing (see Activity 39 – The First Aid Kit) as they walk if they want or some pupils count their steps and (2) broadening attention – that is, actively looking at the world around them as they go. One informal, fun way to encourage a broadening of attention is to ask pupils to make a note of one new thing they see every day.

Again, if they find their attention wandering, not to worry. This is perfectly normal. All they have to do is gently and non-judgementally return their attention to the breath and to the activity of watching the world around them; of being an objective observer rather than an introspective tangle of stress.

Relentlessly Emphasise Do-ability

You will know that there's an inherent difficulty to coaching and supporting pupils in this stress-busting mindfulness stuff: the weary cynicism of the teenager. Those guys know everything, so it's often hard to suggest new ways of doing things or unusual ideas to try.

We've learned two things. First, the best way to teach character is by modelling it. Don't underestimate the power of 'I've been trying this recently, and …' as a way of normalising and illustrating the challenges of changing daily habits and routines. That means experimenting with your own and sharing the trials and tribulations as you go. Second, emphasise ease over effectiveness every time if you want to get a habit going. 'This will take you one or two minutes every day' is way better than 'If you spend just an hour every morning …'

To this end, the opening activity in this chapter, The First Aid Kit, suggests three go-to activities for stressed pupils, and each has the time needed to complete the activity.

39. Attitude Activity: The First Aid Kit – Three Exercises to Dissolve Stress

Box Breathing *(Time: 1–2 minutes)*

For this exercise, you need to take four breaths, and as you do so, imagine building a box. Try this once or twice a day, and over a short period you'll begin to feel calmer.

Breath 1: Breathe in through the nose until the lungs are full and the chest is expanded. Take four seconds to fill your lungs. If you want a word in your head to help clear thoughts, the word can be 'right' as you imagine a pen travelling rightwards as it draws the bottom line of the box. Once you're full, hold the breath for four seconds.

Breath 2: Breathe out through the slightly open mouth. Take four seconds to totally empty your lungs. The word 'up' can be mentally repeated here if you need to, as you imagine a line being drawn up to make the right-hand side of the box. When you're totally empty, hold for four seconds.

Breath 3: Breathe in through the nose until the lungs are full and the chest is expanded. Take four seconds to fill your lungs. If you want a word in your head to help clear thoughts, the word can be 'left' as you imagine a pen travelling leftwards across the top line of the box. Once you're full, hold the breath for four seconds.

Breath 4: Breathe out through the slightly open mouth. Take four seconds to totally empty your lungs. The word 'down' can be mentally repeated here if you need to, as you imagine a line being drawn down to complete the box. When you're totally empty, hold for four seconds. You're done!

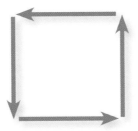

Breath 3: In through the nose, four seconds, then hold for four seconds.

Breath 4: Out through the slightly open mouth across four seconds, then hold for four seconds when empty. Get back to your day!

Breath 2: Out through the slightly open mouth across four seconds, then hold for four seconds when empty.

Breath 1: In through the nose, four seconds, then hold for four seconds.

Deliberate Kindness *(Time: 30 seconds – 1 minute)*

Suggested by a leader at Google, this deliberate kindness exercise takes very little time, but when repeated it has hugely positive effects. Because stress or anxiety is a focus on the self, activities like this work because they require you to place your focus on others.

Version 1

» Choose three people – parents, friends, peers, tutors or teachers, brothers, sisters or cousins.

» Give each of them ten seconds of your time, bringing them to mind, one at a time, as vividly as you can. Mentally say: 'I wish for this person to be happy.' Imagine them happy. Repeat the phrase mentally if you need to for ten seconds.

» Repeat for your three people. That's it.

Version 2

Try this in a public place – a study room, library, cafe, bus station, watching a crowd through a window somewhere.

» Cast your eyes over the crowds around you and choose three random people.

» Give each of them ten seconds of your time, one at a time, as vividly as you can. Mentally say: 'I wish for this person to be happy.' Imagine them happy. Repeat the phrase mentally if you need to for ten seconds.

» Do it for three people. You're done.

When repeated, this exercise trains your brain to spend just a little time focusing on others. Writer, teacher and entrepreneur Tim Ferriss says the following in his book *Tools of Titans* (2017, p. 159): 'I tend to do a single 3- to 5-minute session at night, thinking of three people I want to be happy, often two current friends and one old friend I haven't seen in years. A mere three days into doing this … I found myself wondering throughout the day "Why am I so happy?" … you easily get caught in the whirlpool of thinking about your "stuff". This loving-kindness drill takes the focus off you entirely – which, for me, immediately resolves at least 90% of the mental chatter.'

Concern vs. Control *(Time: 10 minutes)*

This activity, adapted from Stephen Covey's excellent book *The 7 Habits of Highly Effective People* (1989), asks you to spend five minutes or so listing the things that are taking up your mental space and energy. Here's what you do:

1. Listen to your anxieties and worries (your 'mental chatter' as Tim Ferriss calls it) and write it all down – for example, 'worrying about the news', 'worrying about what questions might appear on my next exam', 'stressing about what people might think of my recent post on social media', 'thinking about ice cream'.

2. Put them all in one big circle, so they look as though they're all jostling around in your head. Now draw a second circle, off to the right or left, away from your head.

3. Next, review every item in the circle that looks like your head, crowded with crazy thoughts and issues, one at a time. For each item, ask yourself, 'What control do I have over this?'

4. If there's something you can do to control the outcome of the worry, it stays in the first circle (your head). Label this circle 'control'. If there's little or nothing you can do to control the outcome of the thought or worry, it leaves your head and goes to the second circle. This is going to be called 'concern' – the things you think about but have little or no influence over.

People who handle stress well minimise the stuff in the 'concern' circle. They practise forgetting about it. They spend their energy on the things in the 'control' circle and make plans. Finish the exercise by deciding *one simple thing* you could do to improve each of the issues/situations in your circle of control.

40. Effort Activity: Pre-Making Decisions

Life is full of decisions. Each day we make thousands; estimates range between 3,000 for young children to something like 35,000 for adults. We all experience something called decision fatigue – a decrease in the quality of our decisions over a long period of decision making. (That's why those decisions we make at 10pm after a full day at school might not be our best!) It's partly because we often spend a lot of our decision making energy throughout the day on small material decisions – whether to buy this chocolate or that chocolate, what to eat for lunch and where to sit, how to spend a small amount of money, which bus to catch home and so on.

Often, our material decisions have taken up a lot of mental energy, leaving our behavioural decisions as unplanned reactions. So when a teacher challenges the quality of your homework, it feels unexpected and you might get angry even though you know you shouldn't. Or a friend asks you to skip an after-school class and you blurt out, 'Yes!' even though you know it's a bad idea.

This activity allows you to anticipate some of those decisions and to 'pre-make' them. Use the decision making energy you've got now to plan out responses to future events, and make decisions now that represent the best possible future you.

First, consider these questions:

» What kind of person do you want to be?

» What qualities do you want to have?

» What's important to you?

» What do you want other people to say about you?

» What ideals do you want your strong, confident decisions to be based on?

Scribble down some notes and bear them in mind as you put yourself into some difficult scenarios. Some of them happen to everybody, and we've included them below. Others might be specific to your situation, so there's blank space lower down for you to add your own scenarios.

Scenario	Pre-made decision
You plan on doing some important research but your internet connection is down.	
You set aside some time to catch up on some crucial work but a friend arrives and wants to hang out and chat.	
It's one week until an important test and you know you've got a significant amount of revision to do.	
You're planning on working but a friend tries to persuade you not to.	
You have important tasks you want to get finished but there is something great on TV/social media/the internet.	
A fellow pupil asks you to cheat on a test.	
A friend asks you to skip a class with them.	
A close friend suggests grades aren't that important – that revision is boring and school is worthless. They ask you to join them in quitting study and deliberately failing all exams.	

You can even add situations that help you to pre-decide even more crucial decisions. Think about how you would like the best version of you to respond if, for example, someone offers you drugs or you see a group of people mistreating someone.

You might not always make decisions that fill you with pride, but pre-making good decisions does make them more likely to happen!

12. Coaching with VESPA

The 'What' of Coaching

Coaching is a word used to describe the process of running structured conversations with the aim of, to use John Whitmore's (2009, p. 10) phrase, 'helping [people] learn, rather than teaching them'. Because coaching does not require subject-specific expertise, it can be taken on by tutors and intervention managers who might not know the specifics of performance in maths, computer science or geography, for example, but who can be effective at guiding and developing learners' responses to challenges or obstacles. (Again, Whitmore puts it neatly: 'Good coaching can and should take the performer beyond the limitations of the coach's own knowledge' (2009, p. 12).)

A good coach creates an environment in which pupils feel trusted and supported; a safe space for them to honestly discuss their personal strengths and capacities as well as their foibles, weaknesses or personal barriers. Responsibility for generating and implementing change is handed over to the pupil. This is crucial. They are, this is Whitmore again, 'trusted, allowed, encouraged and supported to make their own choices and decisions' (2009, p. 19). Whitmore argues that offering the learner more choice is a key way of 'unlocking all kinds of hidden potential'. He goes on to suggest that this approach 'builds self-reliance, self-belief and confidence, and self-responsibility' (2009, p. 33, 35).

In coaching conversations we've observed – indeed, in ones we've run, particularly in the earlier days of practice – the teacher does most of the talking and it's usually the teacher who offers their thoughts on how they think the pupil is working and how they should improve. This isn't how coaching is supposed to work, of course. It takes time to master but good coaching is about influence not control. It should help to build a pupil's self-belief, self-confidence and self-responsibility. Ultimately it's about building self-awareness. As noted by Whitmore (2009, p. 37), 'When we truly accept … responsibility for our thoughts and our actions, our commitment to them rises and so does our performance.'

So the key principle of coaching is to unlock the pupil's potential, encourage them to take ownership and responsibility for their performance, and help them to maximise their chances of success – that is, to guide them to a series of actions that will help them to achieve their goals. There is evidence to suggest that coaching pupils can have a positive impact (Campbell and Gardner, 2005). However, there is a caveat: the

National Foundation for Educational Research says, 'Evidence of direct impact on young people from mentoring and coaching within their organisation is rare. However, reports from researchers and teachers suggest that a culture of mentoring and coaching will, over time, have an impact on young people and their learning.'*

The 'How' of Coaching – Making the Time

We've found that one of the biggest barriers to coaching in schools is finding the time to do quality coaching sessions. This can be tricky. Our success with coaching has mainly been with one-to-one conversations or small intervention groups at GCSE and A level. If you're interested in testing out a coaching conversation, here's a way you might do it.

The activity which follows is adapted from *The A Level Mindset*. We suggest that you run this activity after a two or three week block of teaching, giving pupils about twenty minutes of class time to complete it.

* See https://www.nationalcollege.org.uk/transfer/open/mentoring-and-coaching-core-skills/mccore-s02/mccore-s02-t05.html.

Systems Activity: The Weekly Review

Your productivity – the amount of efficient and effective work you do – can be significantly changed by doing your work regularly and often, rather than clearing big piles of it.

Here's a habit to work on developing. It's called the learning review. Follow these steps and you'll find yourself snacking – checking your learning regularly – instead of bingeing!

1. You've got twenty minutes to spend in quiet study and reflection. During the twenty minutes, you're going to review all the work you've completed in the last two to three weeks. Make sure you've got it all in front of you now.

2. Now look through your notes, reviewing the last few weeks' worth of work. Do the following:

   » Check your notes are clear, legible and in order.

   » Summarise your learning in a quick diagram, mind-map or a few lines of notes.

   » Highlight or circle stuff you've found hard during this period. This is the material you'll need to work on during your independent study time.

   » Go through the jobs you've been given over the last two to three weeks, and the deadlines you've got. Make a prioritised list for the fortnight ahead.

People who make a habit of regular reviews like this are often much calmer and less stressed. They can leave school on Friday knowing they're on top of things. They've emptied their heads of all the little niggling worries that might keep them awake at night.

That could be you too! Try building in a learning review on a weekly basis to clear your mind and get your head straight.

Set this activity up, then when the classroom is quiet and the pupils are absorbed in reviewing their own learning, you can select a small group of pupils to sit with you and take part in a coaching conversation. We've suggested a three-part model that takes around fifteen minutes to complete in total.

Stage 1: Diagnosis

(Time: 5 minutes)

Frame the purpose of the conversation. You can go positive and collective: 'I'm checking in with groups of pupils to see how they're getting on. I'd like us to investigate – as a class – a range of different ways of working so that we all learn from each other and do as well as possible! In particular, I want to focus on some of the obstacles you feel you're facing at the moment.' Or you can go for performance-based intervention: 'Recently, I've become concerned that you're not meeting the standards necessary for success this year. I want to help you make some changes that will impact positively on the way you're approaching your studies at the moment.'

Then establish motive: 'What grades would you like to achieve by the end of your GCSEs?' as well as current reality: 'What are you finding hard about GCSE study in this subject?' Often, this question alone will be enough to encourage discussion. If not, use the question tables which follow to go deeper. Keep the pronoun as 'you'; there's no reference to 'I' here as the emphasis is entirely on the learner. Narrative question stems often work well: where analysis can be challenging ('Why are you finding this subject hard?'), storytelling is a more natural mode ('Tell me the story of a lesson you found hard recently …').

Watch out for false reality syndrome – the tendency for some pupils to tell you what they think you want to hear. Keep an eye out for emotive, self-critical or judgemental language used by pupils. Diffuse it. Instead, go for facts and figures. Try to build a detailed, non-judgemental description of the pupil's performance. Where are their areas for development?

Our intervention conversation will flag up one (usually more, sometimes five!) area for concern. Once we've diagnosed, we have to decide where to begin. There are various ways of considering this. If a pupil is in crisis, we'll naturally need to start where the tension is – the root cause. Often this is vision. The process could be long but it will be worth it. Alternatively, if we're making smaller, incremental adjustments to performance, we might begin at the point where we can make either the quickest change or the highest impact change for the lowest cost.

We recommend that in your first session you only work on one or two areas. If you try to change too many behaviours at the same time, it's likely you will fail. Behaviour change is often about altering habits, and these are more likely to stick if done in small steps. The process from there is about selecting VESPA activities that can practically and measurably change pupil behaviour. Which tool you use will quite often depend on your professional judgement about what you think might work best with the individual pupil. You can either work through the VESPA tools with the pupil or you might ask them to complete a task at home and bring it back with them to the next session.

Stage 2: Planning and Modifying Planning

(Time: 5–7 minutes)

Shift the emphasis from 'you' to 'we'. You're a team now, supportive, with unified goals: 'How can we work together to improve matters?' 'Can we come up with a plan that will make things better?' 'What might we do to get past this barrier? Any ideas?'

The aim, to use Whitmore again, is 'not to find the right answer but to create and list as many alternative courses of action as possible' (2009, p. 79). So, non-judgementally, begin to scribble down possible courses of action, nudging and encouraging wherever you can, but resisting the attempt to dominate and provide all the answers. Good prompts here might be: 'Is there anyone who could help us, do you think?' 'Who do we know that might have overcome this problem before?' 'Let's give it a few more minutes to try to generate another idea or two.' If they dry up offer ideas of your own, but only with their permission. Try: 'I think I might have a couple more possible solutions. Anyone want to hear them?'

We're fond of using The Action Priority Matrix (Activity 37) to assess all our ideas once they're generated. Alongside the pupils, assess which solutions are the lowest effort, highest impact solutions, and choose the best one. We much prefer coaching sessions that recommend the use of a VESPA activity as a tool to structure a plan and a commitment, but that's just us.

Stage 3: Commitments

(Time: 3–4 minutes)

The emphasis returns to the individual now, and 'we' is replaced by 'you': 'So, which of these possible solutions are you going to choose?' 'What are you going to be doing before we next meet?' 'How are you going to do this?' 'What will you need to do first?'

Tempting as it might be to own solutions together, the actions *must* belong to the pupils. Avoid softening responsibility now with collective pronouns ('we' or 'our') which blur the clarity on who is doing what, or hedges like 'perhaps', 'might' or 'maybe'. You're going for optimal clarity and commitment to action, so this sort of comment is to be avoided: 'So before we meet again, let's consider how we might review our notes more regularly, OK? And perhaps we can submit that extra piece of work we mentioned?'

Recording the Conversation

There are different views about recording coaching conversations. A simple record of your conversation should be your aim. This is important so that when you evaluate the

pupil's progress, you also have some notes and a record of the agreed action steps. The more stakeholders, the greater the sense of accountability on the part of the pupil. A formal record of what has been agreed therefore works well – perhaps a list of actions that can then be shared with parents or, if an early intervention, with tutors, heads of year or heads of department.

As an alternative to Four Steps Forward – which we like as a pupil record for recording solutions and possible ways forward – something as simple as the record sheet below will help tutors and teachers hugely.

	Notes	Action steps/tools	Priority
V			
E			
S			
P			
A			

Monitoring, Evaluation and Modification

Like any good coaching conversation, you are aiming to end your first session with time-bound targets that can be discussed at your next meeting. Pupils need to leave the meeting with a clear, unequivocal record of their action steps. If they don't, all you've done is 'have a word'!

Your subsequent aim is to catch pupils doing things right and begin celebrating those small steps forward. In order to do this effectively it's important to give your pupils some time to change their behaviour. Through this period you simply monitor their performance. It's important that you have accurate and reliable tools for monitoring progress or it will be difficult to observe any changes. Use attendance, punctuality, behaviour logs, work submission and teacher feedback.

The time you leave between coaching sessions will depend on the pupil's issue(s). We recommend two weeks as a maximum. During the second conversation you review how things have been going and then modify the plan. If things have gone well, and you feel confident that the issue has been resolved, then the pupil might exit the intervention. If not, then you review the action steps and repeat the process using the VESPA tools. Depending on the pupil, this will usually determine the number of coaching sessions

you have. We have had success with pupils after one session, whereas others have taken four or five.

Whatever the outcome, stick at it. Remember that coaching, like developing skills and habits, is a long game. It might not beat micromanagement to begin with, but long term it will reap huge benefits. For us, there's always an inflection point – a moment where a pupil clicks, masters an element of their study and makes a significant step forward. Carol Dweck's persistent use of the word 'yet' in her 2014 TED Talk, 'The Power of Believing That You Can Improve', is a reminder to us all that mastery takes time. Don't label a young person by using language which doesn't allow for the possibility of change. Avoid 'You're disorganised'; go instead for 'You haven't yet mastered some of the methods which will boost your levels of organisation.' 'Yet' offers up a world of possibilities. Your coaching conversations should do the same.

VESPA Coaching Questions

Asking great questions is key to unlocking self-awareness in pupils. By asking pupils questions that really make them think, the hope is that you will break down barriers and encourage them to take responsibility. Below are some example VESPA questions that you could use during any discussion or coaching conversation. (Many thanks to all the staff who have, over a period of time, helped us to develop these, particularly staff at Notre Dame College in Leeds who enthusiastically and perceptively began the process of generating and categorising possible VESPA questions.)

Vision
What do you want to do next? What if you don't get the grades? What other options are there?
Where do you see yourself in ten years' time?
What do you want to achieve in the next year?
What would be important to you in a job?
What is most important for you this year?
What things do you *not* want to be doing in two years' time?
Imagine you are 25. When you wake up in the morning, what does your perfect day look like?
What is your favourite subject/which subject do you enjoy most?
What obstacles do you think you may have to overcome while at school?
What do you wish for in life?
What would be the best you will achieve after school?
How much do you think you are wanting to achieve for yourself or for other people?
Do you compare yourself to other people (envy/jealousy)? Who would you like to be?
What stage of your life are you most looking forward to?
What's the worst that could happen if you don't _____?
Who do you admire most and why?

Effort

How many hours a week of independent study do you currently do?

How many hours have you studied for *this week* outside the classroom?

Do you think you are working hard enough?

How much work would you have to do in order to feel satisfied?

When working, how do you know you have done enough?

Do you think you could spend more time studying?

Do you work more or less than your friends?

Do you think you make enough effort in _____?

What amount of effort deserves a reward?

What is your best time of day for working?

If you had an extra hour every day, how would you end up spending it?

Which subject do you work the hardest on? Why do you think this is?

Is your goal achievable with your present effort?

Are you working as hard for your GCSEs as you did in Year 7, 8 or 9?

How much time do you spend on other activities – why?

In an average week, how many hours do you study at home? How many of those hours are spent on hard/challenging/uncomfortable work?

Name a pupil who works harder than you. What do they do?

On a scale of 1–10, how much effort are you putting in?

What would make you increase your effort?

For your last homework, was your objective to (a) complete it quickly, (b) get the best grade or (c) avoid doing it?

Systems

If you could change one aspect about the way you work, what would it be and how would you change it?

How do you feel on a Sunday night – ready for the work ahead or not?

How do you prioritise what needs to be done?

On a scale of 1–10, how would you rate yourself in terms of organisation?

What do you think you need to do to improve your organisation?

Do you have a workspace in which to do your work?

Describe your workspace.

How do you ensure your work is up to date?

Are you spending more time on one subject than the others? Why?

How do you follow up the classwork done during the day?

How do you prepare for the next lesson?

In what area (home or school) are you most organised?

Show me a file you are proud of.

Suggest one thing that prevents you from being organised.

How do you record homework tasks?

How do you know what work is currently outstanding?

Do you have a study plan for the week/month/term?

What do you use to make sure you meet deadlines?

How could you create an extra hour every day to use in a productive way?

Think of one thing you could do this minute to improve your organisation.

Practice

If you do past paper questions, do you ever self-mark them?

Where do you go to access support?

In your studies, how do you feel/react when you have made a mistake?

Do you tend to focus on/practise the content that you enjoy?

Do you access exam papers or mark schemes as part of your revision? What revision materials do you use/produce?

Do you review your work to make it better?

When was the last time you tested yourself?

When did you last ask someone else to test you?

How do you practise your key skills in _____?

How do you revise?

Describe your response to the last disappointing grade you received.

What do you do with your homework when it is a low grade?

What do you do with the feedback you get on marked work?

If you could pick one activity to use to revise for an exam, what would it be?

How many times have you read the feedback on work in _____?

How do you respond to feedback?

If you've got one hour, and no homework, what would you do to help your learning in _____?

Is every mistake you make a bad thing? What have you done differently after making a mistake?

How do you improve your work after it's been graded?

How would you describe a thirty minute revision session in your house?

Pick one of your subjects. Which aspects of this subject do you least need to revise? Why?

Attitude

How do you feel when you get something wrong?

What do you do when you encounter a problem?

Do you think you're in control of your life, or is it just fate/chance?

How do you respond when you get work back?

Do you mind how you look in front of other pupils?

Are there any people who are stopping you from achieving?

When something goes wrong what do you do?

What's the biggest mistake you have made so far? What have you learned/how did you deal with it?

Tell me about a time you had to start something again from scratch. How did you feel at the time? How about once it was done?

What have you done since September that you are proud of?

Describe your most challenging subject. Why? What do you do about it?

How do you respond to setbacks?

How do you respond to not getting the grade that you want?

Describe a moment when you felt proud.

What do you do to make yourself feel better?

What do you feel is the difference between you and an A grade pupil? List five.

If you get a poor grade, what do you do to make sure it doesn't happen again?

Think of something you're good at. Tell me how you became good at it.

How would you advise your friend if they got a very low grade?

When you don't get the best mark, how does it make you feel?

Name something you have persevered with in the past.

How do you feel when you fail a test?

What would you do if you got grade E on an assignment?

Is it possible to improve after your mock exam grade?

How do you learn from your mistakes?

What advice would you give to a younger brother or sister who wasn't reaching their goals?

13. Implementation

Putting VESPA into Action

> The sensible question to ask about a school's character education strategy is not, therefore, whether such education does occur, but whether it is intentional, planned, organised and reflective, or assumed, unconscious, reactive and random.
>
> Jubilee Centre for Character and Virtues (2017), p. 2

The quote above is worth reflecting on. In your classroom or school, is your strategy for developing non-cognitive skills, habits and behaviours 'intentional, planned, organised and reflective' or 'assumed, unconscious, reactive and random'? Many schools we work with claim that they are developing pupils' essential skills, but when asked to be explicit about the 'how' they often struggle to show that they have a well thought through strategy.

There are generally two schools of thought on developing non-cognitive skills, usefully expressed as caught versus taught. One view is that they are 'caught' through role modelling and school culture; the other view is that they should be taught using specific activities.

We reckon the Jubilee Centre's Demos report nails it when they argue that non-cognitive skills and habits are '"largely caught through role-modelling and emotional contagion" so "school culture and ethos are therefore central"', but – and this is crucial – that '"character should also be taught" because "direct teaching of character provides the rationale, language and tools to develop character"' (Birdwell et al., 2015, p. 11).

So how can non-cognitive skills and habits be taught? For us, two main vehicles have presented themselves and we've used them both. The first is through a fundamental redesign of the pastoral curriculum so that tutorials, study sessions and assemblies are used to teach non-cognitive skills and habits. This is explicit, macro level education that a whole key stage might engage in. The second is through focus groups, action research and coaching interventions with targeted cohorts or one-to-one situations (i.e. the micro equivalent). The micro approach is for the classroom teacher or middle leader who would like to try out a VESPA intervention with a small group. The macro approach is aimed at the senior leader who may be responsible for leading this type of project across a whole school. More on the two approaches later. (We've

kept both approaches fairly straightforward and simple. There are far more detailed books on project and change management out there if needed.)

Before we consider the specifics of implementation, there are some key questions that need some further exploration.

What Do Sessions Exploring Non-Cognitive Skills Look Like?

Teaching a set of habits, skills and strategies is not like teaching maths or history. If the simple provision of information was all it took, our assemblies covering growth mindset, grit and the 10,000 hour rule would have translated into immediately changed pupils. (We can't speak for you, but ours didn't.)

Rather than a chunky hand-out detailing evidence drawn from academic studies, pupils need time and space to (perhaps not in this order!) cynically reject material, process it more subconsciously, reconsider it, reflect on their current practice, develop self-awareness, experiment with a variety of new tools and strategies and, finally, choose the tools and approaches they feel will have the most positive impact for them.

With that in mind, the activities in this book are intended to be subtle nudges that initiate new ways of thinking, behaving and operating. There isn't a single one that will be a game changing silver bullet for every pupil in your cohort. This can be a frustratingly unfamiliar experience for some staff. They're used to teaching a topic and confirming their success by testing understanding ('They all get it. Great!'). Psychological interventions don't work this way. Instead, frame it like this: 'Every single activity you lead could make a massive, life changing difference to two or three pupils. The following session might open a door for another two or three.' Kids need to know this, and staff need to know this too.

Your aim, therefore, is to present a number of tools non-critically and develop pupils' self-awareness by allowing them to experiment and decide what works best for them. It's about providing a toolkit for learners to open and root through when they hit a sticking point, and giving them a small number of exposures to these tools, guiding them in their use. Often coaching interventions are too brief and isolated on the one hand, or repeated so often on the other that pupils begin to feel as though they're special cases, struggling to come to terms with Key Stage 4 study. David Yeager and Gregory Walton from the University of Texas summarise 'psychological interventions' well when they note that 'the teaching of academic content in school is fundamentally different from the delivery of psychological interventions. Academic content is complex and taught layer upon layer: the more math pupils are taught, in general the more math they learn. Changing students' psychology, by contrast, sometimes requires a lighter touch' (Yeager and Walton, 2011, p. 21).

What exactly does a 'lighter touch' mean?

Our answer (emerging from our context, of course – the pupils we worked with and the systems within which we had to work) was around twenty minutes a week for a planned activity (the macro), with bespoke interventions when necessary (the micro).

This was our starting point. Close to five years later, we were approaching a point where VESPA had worked its way into the fabric of the school's culture. This can happen for you too; eventually, teachers will use the model when working with their tutor groups, when coaching their pupils and hopefully within lessons. Its impact is exponential; slow at first, but gathering momentum as you go.

Light Touch, Long Game

Teaching essential life skills is a long game. You'll be faced with some staff – perhaps even senior leaders – who want immediate and measurable impact. We've had conversations like this before: 'I can appreciate how VESPA works and what it provides. But what will it do to our A*–B percentage this summer?'

This is frustrating and misses the point. Let's take a moment to examine the specifics.

First, a significant part of our responsibility at any key stage is to ensure successful transition to the next stage. According to the Higher Education Statistics Agency, in 2014/2015 year one university drop-out rates rose (again) from 6% to 6.2%.* Pupils from disadvantaged backgrounds drop out at a higher rate of around 8% each year, and at the time of writing this figure was also increasing. It's important to consider these figures for a moment: they might be describing *our* ability (or otherwise) to get pupils university-ready. There are a number of experimental studies that have shown that even brief psychological interventions (in some cases, very brief) can lead to long lasting changes in mindset (Yeager and Walton, 2011) and, by extension, behaviour. So we might not see immediate and measurable changes in A level grades in the first year of a psychological intervention, but we might instead look forward to the prospect of young people having more successful and productive university experiences.

Second, in a world addicted to instant impact and immediate gratification, schools often abandon interventions deeming them unsuccessful because they either (a) haven't run them for long enough and allowed the impact to accrete or (b) measured the wrong thing and come to false conclusions.

Changing mindsets means changing the ways in which pupils conceive of themselves and the world around them. In most cases, a single session won't do that; repeated exposures stand a much better chance. Cohen and Sherman's (2014) suggestion about designing effective psychological interventions is helpful here. They recommend using small interventions to change how people understand themselves. So, if you really want to develop the mindsets of your pupils you are going to need some grit, perseverance and resilience to see it through.

It's important to remember that, quite often, you are starting from scratch with the teachers involved in these projects and they also need time to develop their skills and refine the delivery of the interventions. Psychologists often talk about the time paradox in sport. This is the theory that great sports people are able to read 'the subtle queues of their opponents, extracting information about their intentions through early-warning signals (posture orientation, tiny alterations in body language etc.)' (Syed, 2017, p. 87). We would argue that it's the same for teachers delivering these types of intervention. It takes time to develop this level of awareness. In the early stages

---

* See https://www.hesa.ac.uk/data-and-analysis/performance-indicators/non-continuation-summary.

there will be little impact on grades – which are a blunt, insensitive tool that can't hope to measure the small, gradual improvements that habitual change brings about. So watch out for the staff member who says, 'We ran this intervention for the summer term and there was no change to the number of pupils getting top grades,' and therefore arrives at the conclusion that the intervention didn't work.

This brings us to the third issue: what if we're measuring the wrong thing? What about qualitative data? Ask pupils if they feel better supported, better able to solve problems, more confident in their time management, more positive about their education, whether they're enjoying challenges more, whether they're happier with the progress they feel they're making. These are all crucial. Look at attendance at form time, punctuality, behaviour – anything but trying to define interventions purely in terms of the grades they deliver. (That's not to say, by the way, that our interventions didn't deliver better results. They emphatically did; just not straight away.) It's important to remember that rather than some silver bullet, mindset strategies and interventions are 'tools to target important psychological processes in schools' (Yeager and Walton, 2011, p. 293).

Getting Started: The Micro Approach

When individual teachers are testing something in their own classroom or department, what they are usually referring to is undertaking some action research. Action research is simply experimenting with a new teaching or learning strategy, usually on a small scale. This approach is gaining popularity in schools and can provide some really useful evidence and learning before attempting to introduce a project on a larger scale. We've been impressed with Wood and Smith's *Educational Research: Taking the Plunge* (2016) if you want a comprehensive coverage of the research process, but if a shorter, simpler summary suits you, try the following.

Step 1: Clearly Outline the Problem

What is it that you are looking to investigate? It might be useful to just trial a few elements of the VESPA model at this stage, rather than try to develop your pupils on all of the scales. You could use the VESPA questionnaire to identify weak spots (see Chapter 14 for the full twenty-eight-item questionnaire). It's important to use data to help inform the research question. You will also want to have some measures at the start of the research so you can look at the impact post intervention.

Step 2: Design the Intervention

There isn't just one method of delivering the VESPA intervention or a specific time that the intervention has to be delivered in. You might decide to have a specific focus and test it over six weeks, or you might decide to try three elements of the model over a number of months. Either way can work fine. It can be useful to involve others at this point. Share your plan with colleagues and see if they have any suggestions on how it could be improved. A number of schools now have research leads or links to academics that you can ask for advice.

When planning any intervention we've always found that it's useful to consider two important things. First, what is the pupil data telling us? Is there an issue with vision or is it attitude? Second, what is going on in the school calendar during the intervention? Are there likely to be assessments in all subjects or will pupils get reports during the intervention? If they do you can build in activities that might help pupils during these stages. When you've decided on your plan, don't forget to communicate it clearly to your pupils. Let them know what's happening and when – and why. When you've decided on your plan, don't forget to communicate it clearly to your pupils and their parents. We've found we've got additional leverage and buy-in from letters home to parents explaining the project.

The following table is a simple plan for developing vision and attitude with a class over an eight-week block (the school calendar had no significant events during this time).

Step 3: Delivery

During the delivery phase we suggest that you keep some field notes. What's working? What's not working? What would you change? What did pupils say when you were doing the activities? Have you noticed any change in behaviour?

Week 1: Pre-test	Complete VESPA questionnaire. Introduce VESPA model to pupils and an outline of the plan.
Week 2: Vision	Activity 1
Week 3: Vision	Activity 2
Week 4: Attitude	Activity 3
Week 5: Attitude	Activity 4
Week 6: Vision	Activity 5
Week 7: Attitude	Activity 6
Week 8: Post-testing	Completion of the VESPA questionnaire. Measure distance travelled.

Step 4: Evaluation

As you move towards the closing stages of your research, you'll need to consider some post-testing – that is, collecting some data that demonstrates the distance travelled (if any) by the group. This can involve collecting both quantitative and qualitative data, as discussed earlier. Ask the pupils to complete the VESPA questionnaire again and look at any distance travelled. It's also worth getting some feedback from the pupils, perhaps from a small focus group or questionnaire. A word of warning about pupil voice: when it comes to mindset work, pupils don't always know a good thing when they see it. We've had pupils come to us after the exams and say that it was only during this period that they found they needed the strategies and were very glad they had them. Many of the activities are designed to push pupils out of their comfort zone, and this will mean that at times they feel the pain or find it challenging.

Step 5: Write-up

The final stage of your action research is doing a short write-up. Don't keep your findings to yourself – write it up and circulate it. The write-up can be useful, even if things haven't gone to plan! A simple two-page document with the following headings is all you need:

» **Introduction**: give a brief outline of your project. It can be useful to signpost any research you used here.

» **Method**: provide an overview of your plan. What tools did you use? How long did the intervention run?

» **Results**: show your findings. Bar charts can be useful to show your pre- and post-test data. Don't worry about getting caught up with statistical analysis at this point. Remember, this is just a small pilot.

» **Discussion**: how did you find the intervention? What were your learning points?

» **Evaluation**: use the feedback from your pupils here. What did they think? Go back to your field notes and do a brief strengths and weaknesses analysis. Finally, include the next steps. How can the department/school take this forward? Are there tweaks needed or is it something to just ditch? Most research that doesn't show positive results tends not to get published in academic journals; however, you can learn a lot from things that didn't work!

The Macro Approach

In *Making Ideas Happen* (2011, p. 3) (one of our favourite books on project management), Scott Belsky suggests four core components that make an idea happen:

**Making ideas happen =
Ideas + Organisation +
Communal forces +
Leadership capability**

We will try to cover all of these aspects when taking you through the approach suggested here.

Before starting any intervention on a large scale, we suggest that you get a detailed overview of where you currently are.

Step 1: Where Are We? Asking Staff

When we first started trying to figure out how we could help our pupils to achieve their personal best, we asked, why do some pupils fail? When we talk about failing, for us this meant significant underperformance (usually in relation to their target grade). 'Why do pupils fail?' seems like a really simple question but it remains a firm favourite with us because it reveals so much about your staff's conceptions of success and failure, as well as giving them the opportunity to explore the cognitive and non-cognitive reasons for underperformance.

Group your staff carefully, then distribute a whole bunch of sticky notes and ask them to write down one reason why pupils fail their GCSE courses. Be clear on your definition of 'fail': you might mean a specific grade or you might mean significantly underperform relative to target. When your tables are festooned with sticky notes, ask staff to group them into the following categories:

» **Personal issues.** For the most part these are your intractables. Pupils might need involvement from specialists in other agencies or bespoke medical support, for example. There will always be a proportion of these. Set them aside.

» **Cognitive judgements.** Separate out the ones where staff have expressed a personal opinion about pupils, such as 'They're not clever enough'. If the issue is staff mindset, make a note of who you need to convert and start mindset training during team meetings.

What have you got left? It will most likely be observations about pupil mindset: pupils not working hard enough, not being organised, not knowing why they're doing a course or what it's for, or pupils who don't revise properly. When we do training with teachers we find that typically close to 90% of the observations are mindset related. If you want to take it a step further you could do the 'five whys' exercise with some of the observations. It's a simple tool that goes deep into the problem solving process. Here's how it works. You take one of the sticky notes and place it on the board. You then ask for an explanation of 'why' that might be happening. When you have a clearly expressed reason (the pupils aren't sufficiently organised) you ask the same question, 'why?', based on the answer you've just got. You could end up with something like, 'Because we haven't modelled those skills lower down the school!' Often, then, we've found a course of action begins to emerge as you pursue the 'whys'. Asking five whys is considered

Why do we have this issue?

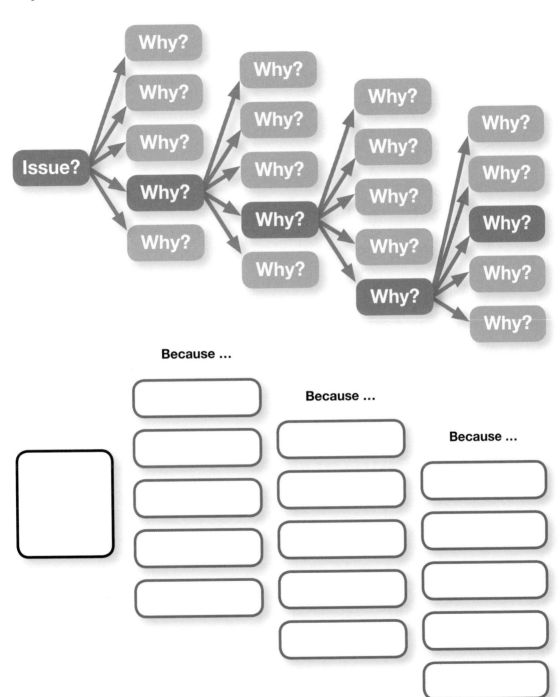

sufficient to dig down into a problem. It can be quite a tricky process but it really makes people think.

Step 1: Where Are We? Asking Pupils

> **Research shows that participation in pupil voice ... can benefit the young people who participate. The Manitoba School Improvement Program found a correlation between an increase in pupil voice ... and an increase in school attachment.** Mitra (2004), p. 653

Dana Mitra at Penn State University has a lot of interesting things to say about the positive impact that pupil voice has on pupil engagement and performance. She looks at three characteristics – agency, belonging and competence – and suggests that active involvement in pupil voice programmes boosts these qualities (Mitra, 2004).

It's well worth organising and running pupil focus groups. There are different ways of doing this. It's possible to do small focus groups or one-to-one interviews. If you are considering a specific mindset intervention, it's best to use a measure that identifies this. You could use the VESPA questionnaire or the grit/growth mindset measures (see introduction). We've found that the guiding principles outlined by Dr Julia Flutter at Cambridge University have worked as a useful checklist when gathering data from pupils

(see Rudduck and Flutter, 2002). Barbara MacGilchrist, Kate Myers and Jane Reed, in *The Intelligent School* (2004), summarise some of the principles Flutter sees as central. For the session to have a positive impact (of the kind suggested by Mitra, above), you need to pay close attention to the following:

» that the desire to hear what young people have to say is genuine;

» that the topic is not trivial;

» that the purpose of the consultation is explained to the young people;

» that young people know what will happen to the data and are confident that expressing a sincerely held opinion or describing a feeling or an experience will not disadvantage them;

» that feedback is offered to those who have been consulted;

» that action taken is explained and where necessary justified so that young people understand the wider context of concerns, alongside their own input, that shape decisions. (MacGilchrist et al., 2004, p. 67)

The VESPA audit

	Focusing	Developing	Establishing	Enhancing
Vision				
Effort				
Systems				
Practice				
Attitude				

The VESPA Audit

The final stage of data collection involves a self-evaluation process; it will help you to review how you are currently developing pupils' non-cognitive skills and to consider the progress you are making with the different scales. We've used a framework suggested by the Jubilee Centre for Character and Virtues in their *Character Education Handbook for Schools* (Harrison et al., 2017, p. 30) (it's a useful read if you'd like to conduct a more thorough audit than we've suggested here). It's probably best to work on this activity as a senior leadership team. For

the categories identified below, decide where you think you are operating and then list some supporting evidence in the table above.

» **Focusing.** The school is beginning to focus on this subheading area. Action is taken to achieve this by the school but it is either minimal, not successful or in its early stages.

» **Developing.** The school is actively trying to develop this subheading area. Action is taken to achieve this by the school and there may be tentative signs of impact in these early stages.

» **Establishing.** Over a designated period of time, there is growing evidence which shows successful implementation of this subheading area within the school's provision.

» **Enhancing.** Over a designated period of time, the school has established an array of evidence which shows successful implementation of this subheading area within the school's provision. The evaluation process places the improvement and enhancement of the provision at the forefront of the school's activity and the school is continually developing and evaluating available evidence. New and innovative ways to meet this subheading are in place or being developed in the school.

Packing Your Bags

Having done a thorough review of where you are, there will be some things that you'll want to take forward with you and some things that are best ditched. When designing a VESPA intervention, don't think that you have to start from scratch and ditch all the great work you've already done. Every school we've worked with has a number of their own VESPA tools that are working really well with pupils.

Packing Your Bags is a simple tool first taught to us during some impressive change management CPD we were lucky enough to gatecrash. Despite its simplicity, it really helped us to reframe our thinking, remember our position of control and decide what to keep and what to discard. We've also found it a great tool to use with staff after running an intervention. For each of the eighty-plus tools we've developed in *The GCSE Mindset* and *The A Level Mindset*, there are a number (too many to even think about) which got left behind.

Pack	Leave behind

Where Do You Want to Go?

Reviewing the data in step 1 will give you a good indication about where you currently are. Do your staff think that pupil mindset is an issue? What is the pupil data telling you? Now that you have a clearer picture of your current context, it can help you to form the research question.

Step 2: The Research Question

When identifying where you want to go, we suggest that you devise a well-framed research question. This will help everyone to be clear about what you are trying to achieve. It will also help you when you come to review the impact. For a GCSE mindset intervention, the question could be: 'Do VESPA tools have any impact on our pupils' mindset?'

Step 3: The Measures

Using appropriate measures is key to identifying the outcome of the project. When we designed the VESPA questionnaire we had two aims in mind. First, we wanted a tool to help us understand how pupils were thinking and behaving. Second, we wanted a tool to measure the distance travelled by pupils on the VESPA scales. The VESPA questionnaire would be an obvious measure to use if you were delivering this intervention; however, using other measures (in addition) can also be useful to triangulate the data. We covered much of this earlier. You could also use some other measures such as attendance, progression and behaviours. There has been some research to suggest that these factors are key indicators of pupils' non-cognitive skills.

In the last chapter we discussed some of the issues with self-reported measures. You won't find it hard to find the critics. Dweck's paper (2015) provides some food for thought. In our experience, if the self-reported questionnaires are administered appropriately they can provide some really useful insights; however, no measure is perfect and your goal should be to try to find the most valid measure for the intended purpose.

Step 4: The Design

We appreciate that most people reading this section will be concerned with whole school development; however, we still recommend that you start with a pilot study. This is a small scale test run of what you might want to do on a larger scale. What your pilot study is allowing you to do is build a prototype. You're getting your innovation out there, watching it fail or succeed and learning the lessons. Make adjustments if it all goes wrong, and do so cheerfully! If something isn't working, and you're confident enough to point it out and remove or change it, your colleagues will see someone who is creative and flexible, someone who isn't pig-headed or precious about a particular idea or way of doing things. The idea of prototyping has proved useful for us because there is a tendency in everyone (us included) to labour in secret, waiting until something is close to perfect before letting anyone else see it. Weeks turn into months,

months into years and 'that project' you've talked about is still in the third drawer down – the graveyard of a thousand good ideas. The size of your pilot depends on what you think is appropriate.

It's now quite common to hear about randomised control trials (RCTs) in education. It's considered the 'gold standard' of research and it's been used in medical research for years. You might think that this isn't necessary if you're not going to publish your research; however, if you want to be thorough it's worth considering. One of the key strengths of an RCT is that it avoids selection bias (like picking your most committed teachers to deliver the intervention). So, in your pilot this means randomly selecting the groups that will be involved in the intervention and those not selected acting as the control group (measured but no intervention).

There are many different categories of randomisation. In a school context it's probably best just to consider two categories: simple or restricted. Simple randomisation is putting all the groups (let's say all Year 11 tutor groups) into a hat and randomly selecting those which will and those which won't receive the intervention. This approach would be fine in most schools; however, if your form groups (or teaching groups if you're delivering the intervention within a department) are in ability groups, you might need to consider restricted allocation. This

involves stratifying the groups so there is balance before randomisation.

So this might look like:

Set 1	Two sets randomly selected	Set 2	Two sets randomly selected
Set 3		Set 4	
Set 5		Set 6	
Set 7		Set 8	

There are plenty of online tools to help with randomisation. It's always useful to get a witness to observe the process as people quite often complain about being in the control group. If you choose this approach you might get asked, 'Is it fair that we have some pupils in the control group?' Our response to this is that until you've tested the intervention in your context you don't know if there's going to be any impact.

If there's pressure on you to deliver an intervention with all pupils and you'd still like to do an RCT, there's one approach left. It's something we've done before with schools and it can work well, but requires more thorough planning and monitoring. For this approach you might work with the whole year group. Rather than have control groups that have no intervention, you randomly allocate elements of the VESPA model to all groups – for example, you might have some groups who just do vision and effort activities and some groups that just do systems and attitude activities. This approach makes the analysis a little tricky but it can be done.

Step 5: The Plan

All those involved need to have a clear sense of what the steps are going to be. We've worked with a number of schools that have invested a great deal of time in the first steps but fail to plan adequately. It's important to devote some time to this. We've found Gantt charts to be a simple and effective way of planning. They provide a clear visual of timelines as well as the tasks that need to be completed. When it comes to communication you probably can't over-communicate regarding the plan. Updates in emails, newsletters and briefings are all useful.

To support the activities being completed in tutorial time, you may want to consider some other whole school approaches that could be utilised to reinforce the messages. Remember, it's not about hitting pupils over the head with the same messages, but subtle reminders can help.

» **Assemblies.** The obvious place to start is assembles. Most schools already have a well-established assembly programme. We're not suggesting any large scale changes here. It's more about considering where messages that reinforce the VESPA model could be included – for example,

Figure 13.1. A simple Gantt chart

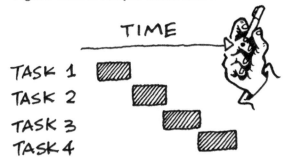

stories around famous people who have shown all the VESPA qualities.

» **Visuals.** If you're a Twitter junkie you'll see that growth mindset posters/displays seem to get a fair bit of negative feedback. We are big fans of these types of displays. If going whole school with the VESPA model, your displays can be used as a cultural transmitter, emphasising key ideas and messages. This doesn't mean bespoke VESPA posters of course – there's plenty of interesting material out there. Don't over-do it; often pupils look past material if it feels ubiquitous or over-used.

» **Celebrations.** It's useful to try to reward pupils in relation to the scales. Letters home emphasising the importance of a specific non-cognitive quality can be really helpful. You might want to try something like this: 'As I'm sure you know, exam success is the result of effort. Students who put in the hours, working diligently and optimistically, are the ones who do best.

With this in mind, I have been keen to praise those students who have worked really hard over the last six weeks or so.

_____ has certainly been one of those students this half-term, and I have made it clear how impressed I've been! Could I ask you to reinforce this praise at home? A positive word, a gesture or a small reward might help reinforce this approach to study for next half-term as well …'

» **Lessons.** The gold standard of any model is to have the messages reinforced in lessons. The Jubilee Centre's Teaching Character Through Subjects programme (see Harrison et al., 2016) is a fantastic example of this. It's not something that we would encourage you to try in the initial stages of the pilot, but it is something to keep in the long-term plan.

» **Parents.** Strangely, in our opinion, parents often don't get informed about mindset interventions. It took us a couple of years to realise the importance of sharing VESPA with parents. It proved to be one of the most constructive steps we took. Parents found the model very easy to relate to and could see straight away where their sons or daughters had areas for improvement. The language between teachers/parents and pupils suddenly became clear!

Step 6: Analysis and Evaluation

Calculating the effect size of your project can seem a little daunting. The Education Endowment Foundation have made this process much simpler by developing an excellent spreadsheet that can be downloaded from their website (there's also a superb DIY evaluation guide that goes with this).* It's important when you're doing the analysis that you examine each of the scales. Don't just look at the overall VESPA score, as this can be misleading.

In addition to looking at the quantitative data, we've always been big fans of collecting some qualitative data. For us this has usually been staff and pupil focus groups. We would argue that this provides you with a more interesting and rounded picture.

Whether you follow the macro or micro approach, all research in schools is tricky and generally messy. Pupils are exposed to a variety of stimuli during their day and it's difficult to pin down the effects of any single intervention; however, we should make every attempt to measure the impact of any intervention that we are exposing our pupils to.

---

* See https://educationendowmentfoundation.org.uk/resources/diy-guide/analysis/.

Seven Obstacles To Watch Out For!

To reiterate: if you expect dramatic changes the first time you try any mindset intervention, you are probably going to be disappointed. It takes time: *developing your class's or your school's approach to mindset is not a quick win!* We usually say to schools that they are embarking on a three-year journey to get the interventions embedded.

It's worth outlining some of the most common problems faced by the schools we've worked with when implementing a mindset programme, so that you can avoid them.

1 **No conceptual framework.** Whether you use the VESPA model or any other model, we feel that it's vital that you have a conceptual model that you use to guide your intervention. When teachers are just delivering 'tools' or 'activities' that are supposed to develop mindset, without understanding the unifying theory behind them, this tends to lead to poor results. It's the explicit links to theory that teachers need to make that quite often develop the pupils' understanding during the activities.

2 **No project manager.** If you're going whole school with any intervention, it needs a project manager – someone who has hopefully volunteered and manages all aspects of the project. Although not essential, our experience has found that it helps if

this is a middle or senior leader. One role of the project manager that we've found has sometimes been overlooked is checking compliance. Rather than observing sessions to ensure they're running as planned and to check quality and share successes, we've seen an assumption that staff will comply without any checks being made. What gets measured gets managed; without any checks, a project like this can fall off the bottom of a teacher's to-do list. You can't draw any meaningful conclusions from a project if you can't confidently prove that it actually happened.

3 **Teachers' fixed mindset.** Before you can start to work on the mindset of pupils, your staff have to be thinking in the right way. Like any proportion of the population, there are a number of teachers who lean towards having a fixed mindset. We've certainly encountered our fair share, and heard it expressed in comments about the pupils they work with. Watch out for comments like these:

» The results are average because the kids are average.

» Give me some good pupils and I'll give you some good results.

» These kids are so weak.

» The requirements of the new GCSE syllabus in *my subject* are huge.

» I'm afraid he's just not a _____ (fill in the gap as appropriate: scientist, linguist, musician, etc.).

» Some have got it, some haven't. This kid hasn't.

» Their backgrounds are so challenging. We can't expect much of them.

Sadly, if a culture develops where comments like these become the go-to explanation for pupil underperformance, no further progress can be made without significant and sustained efforts at cultural change. Instead, the habitual response to disappointing pupil performance is external justifications that can't be challenged or changed. 'It's beyond my control,' the message goes. 'If only we had cleverer kids.' Some serious CPD will be required here.

4 **Staff training.** Teachers need to be trained in the theory and tools. They need to practise using the tools with each other and themselves – adjusting them, redesigning them and owning them – before they can use them really effectively with their pupils.

5 **Poor communication.** You need to communicate with staff frequently about what is happening and when. We've found that recapping the framework in various sessions helps to embed the theory, as does a regular drip-drip of whole school messages via the staff bulletin or briefing papers.

6 **Lack of support.** Don't expect all staff to be fully on board and deliver amazing sessions. Some teachers feel quite uncomfortable delivering these types of interventions; it takes them away from their subject knowledge and they can feel quite nervous in the delivery. It's a good idea to train a group of champions who can help to support teachers in this position.

7 **No follow-up.** Any intervention should have the full feedback loop identified at the start. All the staff involved need to know what is expected of them, how interventions work and what the outcomes have been.

14. Measuring Mindset Using Psychometric Tests

Neil Dagnall and Andrew Denovan,
Manchester Metropolitan University

The VESPA Questionnaire:
A Note from Steve and Martin

We've developed the VESPA questionnaire as a tool for teachers to support the coaching process with individual pupils or to identify areas for development with large cohorts. There are a number of strengths and weaknesses of using this type of measure with pupils, of course. For us, a key point is to remember that this type of questionnaire provides the starting point for a discussion. It should be made explicit to pupils that the questionnaire is being used to support them and help them achieve the best results they can. If pupils feel that they are being measured for some other reason, they are unlikely to offer honest answers. And of course, remember the fluidity of character. The questionnaire will provide a snapshot of how the pupil feels about themselves now. It is not a permanent state that won't yield to development or change.

For the development of the questionnaire, we've been very lucky to have support from Dr Neil Dagnall and Dr Andrew Denovan at Manchester Metropolitan University. Their knowledge and command of their subject has been invaluable and we are grateful for their contribution of this chapter. Neil and Andrew have a high level of expertise; there are sections of this chapter that get pretty in depth and complex.

Dr Neil Dagnall is a reader in applied cognitive psychology. His research interests include parapsychology, anomalous psychology, individual differences and cognition. He can be contacted at: n.dagnall@mmu.ac.uk.

Dr Andrew Denovan is a senior lecturer in psychology. His research interests include stress, individual differences, positive psychology, well-being, parapsychological beliefs and the pupil experience in higher education. He is also interested in research methods such as interpretative phenomenological analysis, psychometrics, statistical modelling and mixed method designs. He can be contacted at: a.denovan@mmu.ac.uk.

What Are Psychometric Tests and Why Use Them?

The term psychometric refers generally to any branch of psychology concerned with psychological measurement. Psychometric tests are standard measures of mental capabilities and behavioural style. Tests assess important individual differences, such as intelligence (ability), skills (aptitude) and personality. To achieve this, psychometric tests employ systematic, standardised procedures to sample ('snapshot') and describe behaviour using scores or categories. An important feature of psychometric testing is that results allow direct behaviour comparison between two or more people.

Psychometrics has a long established tradition within psychology. James McKeen Cattell set up the first dedicated laboratory, Cavendish Physics Laboratory at the University of Cambridge, in 1887. Today the use of psychometric tests is common and widespread. Educators, psychologists and practitioners use tests within a range of vocational and clinical areas, such as teaching, training, recruitment, occupational, clinical and neuropsychology. Historically, education institutions have used psychometric tests for a variety of reasons, but specifically to assess aptitude (entry examinations), ability (pupil strengths and weaknesses) and potential (career possibilities).

More generally, psychologists use psychometric tests to:

» Classify (to select or place people into particular categories).

» Diagnose (to determine reasons for unusual behaviour, with the intention of prescribing appropriate interventions).

» Provide insight (to develop self-knowledge and understanding of individual pupils).

» Evaluate educational/social programmes and develop educational/psychological theory.

The Profiling Approach

Psychometric tests contribute to the development of pupil profiles. Profiles require the accumulation and collation of important information about individual pupils' abilities. In this context, effective profiling charts pupil progress throughout the course of their academic career. Educators use profiles to inform scholastic decisions, particularly as a tool for identifying ways in which to enhance pupil development. Implemented effectively, profiling facilitates educator and pupil management of learning by nurturing a better understanding of pupil ability. Specifically, tests identify strengths and weaknesses which allow educators to appreciate the needs of individual pupils.

In this respect, teachers use profiles to maximise pupil potential and aid progression through important transitions, such as changing year, preparing for GCSEs and moving from GCSEs to A levels. Additionally, psychometric profiling enables comparison of pupil ability via comparisons on relevant comparison (norm) groups. This permits an assessment of pupil ability/potential relative to their peers/classmates. This is invaluable with regard to clarifying individual pupil goals, developmental needs and career aspirations. Finally, profiling can signpost how a pupil is likely to perform in certain educational settings. This information can help to improve self-management in educational and external contexts.

Good Psychometric Tests

Good psychometric tests demonstrate several essential properties – in particular, they must be standardised and objective. To ensure standardisation, trained test administrators follow precise predetermined instructions and protocols. These ensure that test delivery is unbiased and tester beliefs or values do not affect performance. A related requirement is that tests must not discriminate against groups (based on gender, ethnicity, etc.).

Another key feature of good psychometric tests is that they possess reliability and validity. Reliability refers to test consistency (repeatability). In order to provide an accurate indication ('snapshot') of pupil ability, individual test scores must remain stable over

reasonable periods. For instance, accurate weighing scales produce similar readings of a person's weight at different times of day.

There are two main types of reliability:

» Internal (the extent to which test items measure the same construct).

» External (the tendency for a test to produce similar results when repeated).

Both internal and external reliability are vitally important.

Internal reliability is the extent to which a measure is consistent within itself. There are different methods for establishing internal reliability (i.e. split-half and inter-item consistency). The split-half method compares pupil performance on one half of the test with their performance on the other half. It is possible to create halves in different ways (e.g. odd and even numbers, first half and second half). Internal reliability is evident if the two sections provide comparable results. Similarly, inter-item consistency involves assessing relationships between test items to ensure they are measuring the same concept. Similarly, psychometricians use several techniques to assess external reliability (i.e. test-retest and parallel forms). Test-retest involves comparing test performance at two different time points. If scores are similar at time 1 and time 2, this indicates consistency. When pupils sit the same test on more than one occasion they may recall items, hence some tests use parallel forms of analysis. With parallel forms, the comparison derives from test version A and test version B, with alike scores indicating reliability.

Validity is the degree in which a test truly measures the construct it intends to assess. There are a number of ways of establishing test validity. One significant indicator is whether a test has face validity – that is, whether the test appears to measure the construct it claims to assess. A related concept is content validity. Content validity is the extent to which a test instrument samples domain content. This involves considering whether it contains sufficient items to sample the whole construct breadth.

Another important feature of psychometric tests is that they should predict performance. If a test accurately predicts performance on relevant criterion measures then it has criterion validity. This comparison may be concurrent (current) or predictive (future). If a test is valid, it must be reliable. However, reliable tests are not necessarily valid; they may produce consistent scores but not accurately measure the construct of interest.

Benefits of Using a Measure When Working with Young People

Using psychometric tests with young people can aid their development. Psychometric tests allow pupils to better appreciate their abilities (strengths/weaknesses), developmental needs and areas of interest. Results from tests delivered by suitably qualified educators can help to enhance academic performance and behaviour. This is especially true when tests focus on preferred learning and working style. Furthermore, the provision of personalised feedback encourages pupils to engage with and reflect upon learning. Consequently, psychometric tests increase awareness of the degree to which particular characteristics can influence potential success. Ensuing reflection can then form the basis for structuring subsequent learning activities. Applied appropriately, psychometric tests promote understanding of individual differences from both the teacher and pupil perspective.

Psychometric tests can be extremely helpful career wise; results enable pupils to identify areas of aptitude and strength. This information can then help in the setting of goals and provide pupils with focus and purpose. In order to achieve positive outcomes, educators should ensure that pupils receive accurate and suitable feedback. In this context, feedback needs to be constructive and timely. Using feedback to consider educational/vocational choices and inform career possibilities is beneficial and productive to pupil development. The process of review and practice helps to engage pupils in the learning process and moves them from being inactive peripheral learners to active learners at the centre of the educational process.

Pupils should also possess an awareness of the potential limitations of psychometric tests. Principally, they should be aware that tests act only as developmental tools and indicators. Performance may improve with practice and maturation. Additionally, educators need to avoid labelling; test outcomes should not shape expectations of pupil achievement.

Introduction to the GCSE Mindset Questionnaire

Steve Oakes and Martin Griffin devised the VESPA (vision, effort, systems, practice and attitude) system to assist pupil success. They noted that behaviours, habits and attitudes to study were the strongest predictors of pupil success. To determine which attributes were most important they considered factors affecting their pupils and concurrently undertook a literature review. The review identified a number of skills and behaviours. The key was to build these into a quick, engaging and easy to understand teaching model; the purpose being to change the way pupils think, behave and work. After trialling various models, the VESPA model emerged. This focused on five behaviours and characteristics associated with academic success:

» **Vision** – pupils need to know what they want to achieve.

» **Effort** – achievement requires many hours of proactive, independent study.

» **Systems** – in order to be effective pupils must organise their learning time and resources.

» **Practice** – effective learning requires practice to develop skills.

» **Attitude** – success requires pupils to respond constructively to feedback.

Implementation of the VESPA system was successful in the sixth form of The Blue Coat School in Oldham where Oakes and Griffin taught. Over a sustained period grades, attendance and retention increased. While this was not solely attributable to the VESPA system, because the school was generally a well-managed, nurturing and supportive environment, VESPA made a significant contribution.

Noting the success of the VESPA system, Oakes and Griffin developed self-report items to gauge pupil levels within each of the five core behaviours and characteristics. This measure, in the tradition of psychometric tests, once refined and tested, will have the potential to facilitate pupil performance and achievement. To assess the psychometric properties of the VESPA system a twenty-eight-item questionnaire measuring each of the core skills was piloted with 1,669 pupils in the UK (719 boys and 950 girls aged 16–18). The questionnaire included a five-point Likert response scale from 1 (e.g. never) to 5 (e.g. very frequently). To sufficiently cover each aspect of the VESPA system, four questions were devised relating to vision, four questions for effort, five questions for systems, six questions for practice and nine questions for attitude (see Figure 14.1 for the complete VESPA scale).

The statistical properties of the VESPA scale were scrutinised using supported psychometric analytic techniques. First, the internal reliability of the measure was assessed. This was followed by statistical modelling procedures in which the a priori structure of the scale was examined in comparison with the scores of the 1,669 pupils.

The internal reliability was assessed using a statistic known as Cronbach's alpha. This statistic is commonly used as a benchmark to gauge the internal consistency of questionnaires within the field of psychometrics, and an alpha result of 0.7 or greater is viewed to represent sufficient internal reliability. First, the alpha of the total VESPA scale was calculated with a satisfactory result of 0.85. Next, the vision subscale was assessed with an alpha of 0.60, which although is lower than desirable, is just about high enough to be considered acceptable. Effort, attitude and practice reported satisfactory alpha (0.76, 0.78 and 0.73 respectively) and reliability for practice was just below 0.7 with an alpha of 0.67.

The next step was to test whether the a priori VESPA model with its five subcomponents (factors) 'fit' in relation to the responses of the participants. An advanced statistical analysis procedure called confirmatory factor analysis was performed on the data. To gauge 'fit' of the five-factor VESPA model, inferential statistics were considered, which are commonly reported and utilised within the psychometrics literature. These inferential statistics are also known as fit indices and each one comprises a threshold that the results need to meet (similar to Cronbach's alpha). The fit indices were the comparative fit index (CFI), the incremental fit index (IFI), the root mean square error of approximation (RMSEA) and the standardised root mean square residual (SRMR). For a model to be deemed acceptable, CFI and IFI need to be equal to or greater than 0.90, and RMSEA and SRMR need to be lower than 0.08. The five-factor VESPA model fits the data well overall: CFI = 0.90, IFI = 0.90, RMSEA = 0.05, SRMR = 0.05.

Lastly, each of the five factors was inspected in terms of how strongly each question loaded on to its respective factor – for example, how strongly question 3 (a vision question) loads on to a vision factor, how strongly question 28 (an attitude question) loads on to an attitude factor. To determine this, factor loadings for each question were inspected, with a suitable result requiring a loading greater than 0.32 (a commonly accepted criterion within the psychometrics literature). All questions loaded higher than 0.32, with the exception of question 1, and some loaded very highly (greater than 0.7). Overall, these results suggest that the twenty-eight-item VESPA can be considered an internally reliable measure and to comprise five distinct facets of vision, effort, systems, practice and attitude.

Table 14.1. The twenty-eight-item VESPA scale

	Question	Response scale				
		1	**2**	**3**	**4**	**5**
1	I've worked out that attending college/university is a good choice for me.	Strongly disagree	Disagree	Neither agree nor disagree	Agree	Strongly agree
2	I plan and organise my time to get my work done. R	Very frequently	Usually true	Occasionally	Rarely	Never
3	I don't give much attention to my career planning. R	Strongly disagree	Disagree	Neither agree nor disagree	Agree	Strongly agree
4	I complete all my homework on time.	Strongly disagree	Disagree	Neither agree nor disagree	Agree	Strongly agree
5	I stay calm in difficult situations.	Never	Rarely	Occasionally	Frequently	Very frequently
6	I use all my study periods effectively.	Strongly disagree	Disagree	Neither agree nor disagree	Agree	Strongly agree
7	I compare model answers against my own work.	Never	Rarely	Occasionally	Frequently	Very frequently
8	I have a positive view of myself.	Strongly disagree	Disagree	Neither agree nor disagree	Agree	Strongly agree
9	I am a hard working pupil.	Strongly disagree	Disagree	Neither agree nor disagree	Agree	Strongly agree
10	I am confident in my academic ability.	Strongly disagree	Disagree	Neither agree nor disagree	Agree	Strongly agree

	Question	Response scale				
		1	**2**	**3**	**4**	**5**
11	I always meet deadlines. R	Very frequently	Usually true	Occasionally	Rarely	Never
12	I hand in extra exam work for marking.	Never	Rarely	Occasionally	Frequently	Very frequently
13	I bounce back after facing disappointment or failure.	Strongly disagree	Disagree	Neither agree nor disagree	Agree	Strongly agree
14	I strive to achieve the goals I set for myself.	Strongly disagree	Disagree	Neither agree nor disagree	Agree	Strongly agree
15	I summarise important information in diagrams, tables or lists.	Never	Rarely	Occasionally	Frequently	Very frequently
16	I haven't thought about what I want to do when I leave school. R	Strongly disagree	Disagree	Neither agree nor disagree	Agree	Strongly agree
17	I try to spend as little time on my schoolwork as I can get away with.	Very frequently	Usually true	Occasionally	Rarely	Never
18	I take good notes in class which are useful for revision.	Never	Rarely	Occasionally	Frequently	Very frequently
19	If I don't understand class work, I talk to my teacher.	Never	Rarely	Occasionally	Frequently	Very frequently
20	I look forward to taking tests.	Strongly disagree	Disagree	Neither agree nor disagree	Agree	Strongly agree
21	In most classes my main goal is to do the minimum needed so I don't have to work very hard. R	Strongly disagree	Disagree	Neither agree nor disagree	Agree	Strongly agree
22	My books/files are not organised. R	Strongly disagree	Disagree	Neither agree nor disagree	Agree	Strongly agree

	Question	Response scale				
		1	**2**	**3**	**4**	**5**
23	I use mind-maps/diagrams for revision.	Never	Rarely	Occasionally	Frequently	Very frequently
24	When I take a test, I think about how badly I am doing. R	Strongly disagree	Disagree	Neither agree nor disagree	Agree	Strongly agree
25	I use highlighting/colour coding for revision.	Never	Rarely	Occasionally	Frequently	Very frequently
26	Your intelligence is something about you that you can't change very much. R	Strongly disagree	Disagree	Neither agree nor disagree	Agree	Strongly agree
27	No matter who you are, you can change your intelligence a lot.	Strongly disagree	Disagree	Neither agree nor disagree	Agree	Strongly agree
28	It doesn't matter how hard you work – if you're not clever, you won't do well. R	Strongly disagree	Disagree	Neither agree nor disagree	Agree	Strongly agree

Note: R means the item should be reversed prior to calculating usable scores.

To obtain totals for each subscale, do the following: vision – add 1, 3, 14, 16; effort – add 6, 9, 17, 21; systems – add 2, 4, 11, 18, 22; practice – add 7, 12, 15, 19, 23, 25; attitude – add 5, 8, 10, 13, 20, 24, 26, 27, 28.

Pupil Record

On completion of the questionnaire pupils can use the table below to calculate their results. The reverse questions need to have their scores changed; this needs to be made explicit to pupils if they are doing their own calculations.

Table 14.2. Calculating VESPA scores

Vision	Score
Question 1	
Question 3: 5 = 1, 4 = 2, 3 = 3, 2 = 4, 1 = 5	
Question 14	
Question 16: 5 = 1, 4 = 2, 3 = 3, 2 = 4, 1 = 5	
Score = 1 + 3 + 14 + 16 ÷ 4	
Effort	**Score**
Question 6	
Question 9	
Question 17	
Question 21: 5 = 1, 4 = 2, 3 = 3, 2 = 4, 1 = 5	
Score = 6 + 9 + 17 + 21 ÷ 4	
Systems	**Score**
Question 2: 5 = 1, 4 = 2, 3 = 3, 2 = 4, 1 = 5	
Question 4	
Question 11: 5 = 1, 4 = 2, 3 = 3, 2 = 4, 1 = 5	
Question 18	
Question 22: 5 = 1, 4 = 2, 3 = 3, 2 = 4, 1 = 5	
Score = 2 + 4 + 11 + 18 + 22 ÷ 5	
Practice	**Score**
Question 7	
Question 12	

Question 15	
Question 19	
Question 23	
Question 25	
Score = 7 + 12 + 15 + 19 + 23 + 25 ÷ 6	
Attitude	**Score**
Question 5	
Question 8	
Question 10	
Question 13	
Question 20	
Question 24: 5 = 1, 4 = 2, 3 = 3, 2 = 4, 1 = 5	
Question 26: 5 = 1, 4 = 2, 3 = 3, 2 = 4, 1 = 5	
Question 27	
Question 28: 5 = 1, 4 = 2, 3 = 3, 2 = 4, 1 = 5	
Score = 5 + 8 + 10 + 13 + 20 + 24 + 26 + 27 + 28 ÷ 9	
VESPA score	**Score**
Vision	
Effort	
Systems	
Practice	
Attitude	
Score = V + E + S + P + A ÷ 5	

If you are working with a large group of pupils (and you have some administrative support), it can be really useful to put the data into a spreadsheet. This will allow you to drill down into specific elements of the model – for example, who are your low effort pupils? This helps to target specific interventions if needed. You can then start to get quite sophisticated with your analysis. We've found it useful to include other data such as attendance, progress and behaviour records.

Figure 14.1. Example of VESPA scores spreadsheet

Name	Gender	Vision	Effort	Systems	Practice	Attitude	VESPA score
Stefan	m	1	3	1	2	5	3
Sue	f	1	3	2	2	4	2
Aisha	f	2	4	2	3	2	2
Phoebe	f	3	2	3	4	3	3
Jane	f	3	2	3	4	3	3
Amir	m	4	2	3	4	3	3

Conclusion

Ten Final Thoughts

There's far less of a significant link between progress at the end of one key stage and progress in the next than we might suppose. The past doesn't equal the future. That goes for the modest attainer who turns into a breakthrough learner. It goes doubly for the high attainer who expects the same thing to happen again but hits the ceiling.

We believe there are five non-cognitive skill areas and that these five elements – having a vision, making a habit of effort, building effective systems, engaging in high stakes practice and having the correct attitude – can be practised and learned. Here's a useful metaphor to guide your thinking: we're used to the concept of avatars from computer gaming. Games ask us to assume the identity of another character, often a character with certain strengths and weaknesses that need to be upgraded and built upon if we're to be successful. When there is a psychological distance between gamer and avatar, we're happy to go about improving our character – getting more strength here, building intelligence there or developing skills and attributes as the game goes on. When it comes to self-improvement, however, we're way more reluctant and defensive. Learners find it hard to acknowledge and address their weaknesses. Our job is to create a non-judgemental environment in which pupils can

Conclusion

critically assess themselves and support them in making improvements.

On Vision:

1 Having a vision is central to success. But visions don't have to be jobs, careers or even grades – though they can be. Build flexibility into goals by concentrating on purpose and problem: What am I here to help with? How do I want to leave the world a better place? What needs to be accomplished? What makes me feel alive and positive and purposeful? Increasing self-knowledge, even if it's a sense of 'what makes me tick', 'what I like doing' or 'what fascinates me' builds vision. As teachers, we need to remind pupils why they take the courses they do, and how this or that discrete body of knowledge or skill equips our learners to tackle the world around them.

2 Long-term goals are magnetic but we can make short-term goals magnetic too. Don't feel that every pupil needs to know what it's all for straight away. Try monthly or fortnightly goal setting (What would the perfect mock exam performance look like? What actions can we take in the next three weeks to make that outcome more likely?) and reward those milestones when they come.

On Effort:

3 Effort is the product of routine and habit. Recognise that very small, sustained improvements quickly beat huge revolutions in effort that can't be sustained. Remember that as we establish new habits, self-sabotage is the enemy. Even pupils who ascribe problems to external factors likely will be describing internal barriers; study is about mastering the self as much as mastering the subject. Pre-make decisions and actively consider scenarios so that pupils know who they are and the kind of person they want to be. This doesn't guarantee a good decision, but it makes one more likely!

4 Proactive, high effort pupils have (often subconsciously) established for themselves a set of leading indicators (we call them pedometer activities in Chapter 5) that they work on all the time, regardless of teacher instruction. Draw up a list of leading indicator study habits for your course, model how they might be completed, track pupil compliance and reward those who are engaging.

On Systems:

5 To nurture pupils who can sequence and prioritise work, share and model the use of weekly planners (there are a number of examples here and in *The A Level Mindset*). Anyone who's successfully seen through the design and delivery of a big project will have, along the way, developed their own systems and processes for making sure everything gets done by a deadline. But no one teaches us how to do this. Check out any bookshop

and you'll see shelves of self-help guides about productivity and organisation; even as professional adults we sometimes feel overwhelmed by everything we have to do. Clearly planned working weeks can make a huge difference. Pupils are calmer and happier, and lead less cluttered lives.

6 To-do lists are problematic. Every job on the list occupies the same amount of physical space (a line on a page) and by extension the same amount of mental space. The tasks are of equal priority, even when we sequence them. By using matrices, we encourage pupils to see the jobs associated with subjects that are way ahead of schedule and the jobs associated with subjects that are in crisis. The latter need more time and effort directed at them; the former can be finished quickly.

On Practice:

7 Good exam preparation is a three-step process: learning the content, developing the skills and seeking feedback from experts. To be top performers in exams, pupils first need to know the skills being tested. This will allow them to practise under a variety of conditions, building agility and flexibility. Practice can involve isolating the skill and strengthening it over and over again, without the high stakes associated with performing in exam conditions.

8 As teachers we adjust challenge in class, moving pupils out of 'comfort', 'relaxation'

or even 'boredom' into more uncertain territory – 'worry', 'control' or 'potential'. But when they are practising alone, only the best pupils will do this. The majority will design comfortable, non-challenging practice that leaves them bored. We need to show pupils that they can reach zones of potential and flow by gradually raising challenge. Study is intellectual combat. It should feel hard!

On Attitude:

9 Successful pupils have the same number of setbacks and lousy learning experiences as unsuccessful ones – but they've developed a set of psychological tricks, tools and tactics to get them through difficult times. Sharing emotional and psychological maps of challenge will help learners to anticipate and negotiate difficult times. Encourage them to benefit-find – that is, review tough experiences and focus on the lessons learned as a result.

10 Low attitude pupils see the seeking of help as further evidence that they aren't capable of success in a subject or topic. In their minds, they should be able to do it effortlessly alone. Part of the role of the tutor is to help young people audit the full extent of their support network and to help them call in favours. Make as much of peer support as you can, and use Seth Godin's phrase, 'The path is well-lit', a vivid and effective metaphor for illustrating the fact that thousands of

Conclusion

learners successfully travel these roads every single year. Rather than supplying solutions, we should be encouraging consultation, discussion and problem solving by sharing models that encourage consideration of a number of ways forward.

As accountability rises so does our tendency to micromanage the pupil experience. For a host of good reasons, we might find ourselves reducing independent study time, staffing after-school classes, heavily frameworking tasks, reteaching large sections of syllabuses, drawing up contracts – that is, solving every conceivable problem ahead of time for our learners.

But by operating in this way we risk passing on deficiencies. And looking further ahead, for each student who drops out or fails to complete a university course, we create a young person who owes back a chunk of their tuition fees and maintenance loan. And since a larger proportion of non-completers come from disadvantaged backgrounds, we are inadvertently creating debt among those who can least afford it, entrenching social immobility rather than improving it.

Teaching 14–18-year-olds is our *last chance* to give learners the characteristics to successfully tackle learning at subsequent levels. These qualities don't magically appear, however fervently we might hope or expect them to. Instead, pupils need practical guidance, patient support, positive regard and unswerving belief in their ability to reach their potential. Hopefully this book has been able to give you some tools with which to begin the process.

References

Azevedo, R., Ragan, S., Cromley, J. G. and Pritchett, S. (2002). Do different goal-setting conditions facilitate students' ability to regulate their learning of complex science topics with RiverWeb? Available at: http://files.eric.ed.gov/fulltext/ED482509.pdf.

Bandura, A. (1997). *Self-Efficacy: The Exercise of Control* (New York: Freeman).

Belsky, S. (2011). *Making Ideas Happen: Overcoming the Obstacles Between Vision and Reality* (New York: Penguin).

Berkowitz, M. W. and Bier, M. C. (2005). *What Works in Character Education: A Report for Policy Makers and Opinion Leaders* (Washington, DC: Character Education Partnership). Available at: http://www.character.org/uploads/PDFs/White_Papers/White_Paper_What_Works_Policy.pdf.

Berkowitz, M. W. and Bier, M. C. (2006). *What Works in Character Education: A Research-Driven Guide for Educators* (Washington, DC: Character Education Partnership). Available at: https://characterandcitizenship.org/images/files/wwcepractitioners.pdf.

Binet, A. and Simon, T. (1916). *The Development of Intelligence in Children (The Binet–Simon Scale)* (Baltimore, MD: Williams & Wilkins).

Birdwell, J., Scott, R. and Reynolds, L. (2015). *Character Nation: A Demos Report with the Jubilee Centre for Character and Virtues* (London: Demos). Available at: https://www.demos.co.uk/files/476_1505_characternation_web.pdf?1433340847.

Bull, S. (2006). *The Game Plan: Your Guide to Mental Toughness at Work* (Chichester: Capstone Publishing Limited).

Campbell, M. A. and Gardner, S. (2005). A pilot study to assess the effects of life coaching with Year 12 students. In M. Cavanagh, A. Grant and T. Kemp (eds), *Evidence-Based Coaching* (Brisbane: Australian Academic Press), pp. 159–169.

Canfield, J. (2005). *The Success Principles: How to Get from Where You Are to Where You Want to Be* (London: HarperCollins).

Canfield, J., Hansen, M. J. and Kirberger, K. (1999). *Chicken Soup for the Teenage Soul: Stories of Life, Love and Learning* (New York: Vermilion).

Carey, B. (2015). *How We Learn: Throw Out the Rule Book and Unlock Your Brain's Potential* (New York: Random House).

Cepeda, N. J., Vul, E., Rohrer, D., Wixted, J. T. and Pashler, H. (2008). Spacing effects in learning: a temporal ridgeline of optimal retention. *Psychological Science* 19: 1095–1102.

Chambliss, D. F. (1989). The mundanity of excellence: an ethnographic report on stratification and Olympic swimmers. *Sociological Theory* 7: 70–86.

Cirillo, F. (2017). *The Pomodoro Technique: Do More and Have Fun with Time Management* (London: Ebury Publishing).

Clements-Croome, D. and Baizhan, L. (2000). Productivity and indoor environment. *Proceedings of Healthy Buildings 2000* 1: 629–634. Available at: https://www.researchgate.net/publication/237699305_Productivity_and_indoor_environment.

Cohen, G. and Sherman, D. (2014). The psychology of change: self-affirmation and social psychological intervention. *Annual Review of Psychology* 65: 33–71.

Collins, D. and MacNamara, A. (2012). The rocky road to the top: why talent needs trauma. *Sports Medicine* 42(11): 907–914.

Collins, J. (2001). *Good to Great* (London: Random House Business).

Cooper, H. and Good, T. (1983). *Pygmalion Grows Up: Studies in the Expectation Communication Process* (New York: Longman).

Covey, S. R. (1989). *The 7 Habits of Highly Effective People* (London: Simon & Schuster).

Csikszentmihalyi, M. (1997). *Finding Flow: The Psychology of Discovery and Invention* (New York: Harper Perennial).

Csikszentmihalyi, M. (2003). *Good Business: Leadership, Flow and the Making of Meaning* (New York: Penguin).

Dilts, R. B. (1994). *Strategies of Genius*. Vol. 1: *Aristotle, Sherlock Holmes, Walt Disney, Wolfgang Amadeus Mozart* (Capitola, CA: Meta Publications).

Duckworth, A. L. (2013). Grit: The Power of Passion and Perseverance [video]. *TED.com*. Available at: https://www.ted.com/talks/angela_lee_duckworth_grit_the_power_of_passion_and_perseverance.

Duckworth, A. L. (2016). *Grit: The Power of Passion and Perseverance* (London: Penguin Random House).

Duckworth, A. L., Peterson, C., Matthews, M. D. and Kelly, D. R. (2007). Grit: perseverance and passion for long-term goals. *Journal of Personality and Social Psychology* 92: 1087–1101.

Duckworth, A. L. and Yeager, D. S. (2015). Measurement matters: assessing personal qualities other than cognitive ability for educational purposes. *Educational Researcher* 44(4): 237–251.

Dweck, C. (2012). *Mindset: How You Can Fulfil Your Potential* (London: Constable & Robinson).

Dweck, C. (2014). The Power of Believing That You Can Improve [video]. *TED.com*. Available at: https://www.ted.com/talks/carol_dweck_the_power_of_believing_that_you_can_improve.

Dweck, C. (2017). *Mindset: Changing the Way You Think to Fulfil Your Potential* (London: Robinson).

Emmons, R. A. and McCullough, M. E. (2003). Counting blessings versus burdens: an experimental investigation of gratitude and subjective well-being in daily life. *Journal of Personality and Social Psychology* 84(2): 377–389.

Ericsson, A. and Pool, R. (2016). *Peak: Secrets from the New Science of Expertise* (London: Penguin Random House).

Farrington, C. A., Roderick, M., Allensworth, E., Nagaoka, J., Keyes, T. S., Johnson, D. W. and Beechum, N. O. (2012). *Teaching Adolescents to Become Learners: The Role of Non-Cognitive Factors on Shaping School Performance: A Critical Literature Review* (Chicago, IL: University of Chicago Consortium on Chicago School Research).

Ferriss, T. (2017). *Tools of Titans: The Tactics, Routines, and Habits of Billionaires, Icons and World-Class Performers* (New York: Houghton Mifflin Harcourt).

Flavell, J. H. (1979). Metacognition and cognitive monitoring: a new area of cognitive-developmental inquiry. *American Psychologist* 34(10): 906–911.

Flutter, J. and Rudduck, J. (2004). *Pupil Consultation: What's In It For Schools?* (Abingdon: Routledge).

Geirland, J. (1996). Go with the flow [interview with Mihaly Csikszentmihalyi]. *Wired*, (4 September). Available at: https://www.wired.com/1996/09/czik/.

Gladwell, M. (2008). *Outliers: The Story of Success* (London: Penguin).

Glaser, B. and Strauss, A. (1967). *The Discovery of Grounded Theory: Strategies for Qualitative Research* (London: Transaction).

Godin, S. (2015). *Poke the Box* (London: Portfolio Penguin).

Goldberg, L. R. (1990). An alternative 'description of personality': the big-five factor structure. *Journal of Personality and Social Psychology* 59(6): 1216–1229.

Gross-Loh, C. (2016). How praise became a consolation prize [interview with Carol

References

Dweck]. *The Atlantic* (16 December). Available at: https://www.theatlantic.com/education/archive/2016/12/how-praise-became-a-consolation-prize/510845/.

Gutman, L. M. and Schoon, I. (2013). *The Impact of Non-Cognitive Skills on Outcomes for Young People: Literature Review* (London: Education Endowment Foundation).

Harrison, T., Arthur, J. and Burn, E. (eds) (2017). *Character Education Handbook for Schools: Guidance, Approaches and Methods for the Self-Evaluation of Taught and Caught Character Education Provision* (Birmingham: Jubilee Centre for Character and Virtues). Available at: http://www.jubileecentre.ac.uk/1721/character-education/resources/evaluation-handbook-for-schools.

Harrison, T., Bawden, M. and Rogerson, L. (2016). *Teaching Character Through Subjects: Educating the Virtues Through and Within 14 Secondary School Subjects* (Birmingham: Jubilee Centre for Character and Virtues). Available at: http://www.jubileecentre.ac.uk/userfiles/jubileecentre/pdf/TeachingCharacterThroughSubjects/Teaching_Character_Through_Subjects_2016.pdf.

Hassanbeigi, A., Askari, J., Nakhjavanic, M., Shirkhodad, S., Barzegar, K., Mozayyan, M. R. and Fallahzadehg, H. (2011). The relationship between study skills and academic performance of university pupils.

Social and Behavioral Sciences 30: 1416–1424.

Heckman, J. J. and Kautz, T. (2012). Hard evidence on soft skills. *Labour Economics* 19: 451–464.

Heckman, J. J. and Rubinstein, Y. (2001a). *The Importance of Non-Cognitive Skills: Lessons from the GED and Cognition* (Cambridge, MA: National Bureau of Economic Research).

Heckman, J. J. and Rubinstein, Y. (2001b). The importance of non-cognitive skills. *American Economic Review* 91: 145–149.

Holiday, R. (2015). *The Obstacle is the Way: The Ancient Art of Turning Adversity to Advantage* (London: Profile Books).

Ivcevic, Z. and Brackett, M. (2014). Predicting school success: comparing conscientiousness, grit and emotion regulation ability. *Journal of Research in Personality* 52: 29–36.

Jubilee Centre for Character and Virtues (2017). *A Framework for Character Education in Schools* (Birmingham: Jubilee Centre for Character and Virtues). Available at: http://www.jubileecentre.ac.uk/userfiles/jubileecentre/pdf/character-education/Framework%20for%20Character%20Education.pdf.

Jung, Y., Leung, A. and Miller, J. (2016). Do smart students study harder? An investigation of efficient effort among undergraduate university students. *Journal of Economics and Economic Education Research* 17(1): 25.

Khine, M. S. and Areepattamannil, S. (eds) (2016). *Non-Cognitive Skills and Factors in Educational Attainment* (Boston, MA: Sense Publishers).

Kotler, S. (2014). *The Rise of the Superman: Decoding the Science of Ultimate Human Performance* (London: Quercus).

KPMG (2015). Connected cars to deliver huge UK jobs boost, finds first UK study [press release]. *KPMG* (26 March). Available at: https://home.kpmg.com/uk/en/home/media/press-releases/2015/03/connected-cars-to-deliver-huge-uk-jobs-boost-finds-first-uk-study.html.

Landsberg, M. (1996). *The Tao of Coaching: Boost Your Effectiveness at Work by Inspiring and Developing Those Around You* (London: Profile Books).

Landsberg, M. (2003). *The Tao of Coaching: Boost Your Effectiveness at Work by Inspiring and Developing Those Around You* 2nd edn (London: Profile Books).

MacCann, C., Duckworth, A. and Roberts, R. D. (2009). Empirical identification of the major facets of conscientiousness. *Learning and Individual Differences* 47(3): 174–179.

McGeown, S., St Clair-Thompson, H. and Clough, P. (2015). The study of non-cognitive attributes in education: proposing the mental toughness framework. *Educational Review* 68(1). DOI: 10.1080/00131911.2015.1008408.

MacGilchrist, B., Myers, K. and Reed, J. (2004). *The Intelligent School*, 2nd edn (London: SAGE).

McLeod, S. (2013). Kolb – learning styles. *Simply Psychology*. Available at: https://www.simplypsychology.org/learning-kolb.html.

Margolis, H. and McCabe, P. (2006). Improving self-efficacy and motivation: what to do, what to say. *Intervention in School and Clinic* 41(4): 218–227.

Martin, A. J. (2011). Personal best (PB) approaches to academic development: implications for motivation and assessment. *Educational Practice and Theory* 33: 93–99.

Martin, A. J. and Marsh, H. W. (2008). Academic buoyancy: towards an understanding of pupils' everyday academic resilience. *Journal of School Psychology* 46: 53–83.

Mischel, W., Ebbesen, E. B. and Raskoff Zeiss, A. (1972). Cognitive and attentional mechanisms in delay of gratification. *Journal of Personality and Social Psychology* 21(2): 204–218.

Mitra, D. L. (2004). The significance of students: can increasing 'student voice' in schools lead to gains in youth development? *Teachers College Record* 106(4): 651–688.

Moriarity, J., Pavelonis, K., Pellouchoud, D. and Wilson, J. (2001). Increasing student motivation through the use of instructional strategies. Available at: https://eric.ed.gov/?id=ED455962.

Muijs, D. and Reynolds, D. (2011). *Effective Teaching: Evidence and Practice*, 3rd edn (London: SAGE).

Multon, K. D., Brown, S. D. and Lent, R. W. (1991). Relation of self-efficacy beliefs to academic outcomes: a meta-analytic investigation. *Journal of Counselling Psychology* 38: 30–38.

Oakes, S. and Griffin, M. (2016). *The A Level Mindset: 40 Activities for Transforming Pupil Commitment, Motivation and Productivity* (Carmarthen: Crown House Publishing).

Oettingen, G. (2014). *Rethinking Positive Thinking: Inside the New Science of Motivation* (New York: Penguin Random House).

Poropat, A. E. (2009). A meta-analysis of the five-factor model of personality and academic performance. *Psychology Bulletin* 135: 322–338.

Price, A. and Price, D. (2011). *Psychology of Success: A Practical Guide* (London: Icon Books).

Reiss, S. (2000). *Who Am I? The 16 Basic Desires That Motivate Our Actions and Define Our Personalities* (New York: Tarcher/Putnam).

Rohn, J. (1981). Success Leaves Clues [video]. Available at: https://www.youtube.com/watch?v=lCXdTMB4qs8.

Rosenthal, R. and Jacobson, L. (1968). *Pygmalion in the Classroom* (New York: Holt, Rinehart & Winston).

Rudduck, J. and Flutter, J. (2002). *Consulting Young People in Schools*. ESRC Teaching and Learning Research Programme (Cambridge: Homerton College).

Schunk, D. H. (1981). Modelling and attributional effects on children's achievement: a self-efficacy analysis. *Journal of Educational Psychology* 73(1): 203–213.

Schunk, D. H. (2003). Self-efficacy for reading and writing: influence of modelling, goal setting and self-evaluation. *Reading and Writing Quarterly* 19: 159–172.

Schwarzer, R. and Jerusalem, M. (1995). Generalized self-efficacy scale. In J. Weinman, S. Wright and M. Johnston (eds), *Measures in Health Psychology: A User's Portfolio. Causal and Control Beliefs* (Windsor: NFER-Nelson), pp. 35–37.

Seelig, T. (2012). *inGenius: A Crash Course on Creativity* (London: Hay House).

Smith, S. M., Glenberg, A. and Bjork, R. A. (1978). Environmental context and human memory. *Memory and Cognition* 6(4): 342–353.

Stafford, T. and Dewar, M. (2014). Tracing the trajectory of skill learning with a very large sample of online game players. *Psychological Science* 25(2): 511–518.

Stankov, L. and Lee, J. (2014). Quest for the best non-cognitive predictor of student success in college. *College Pupil Journal* 46(3): 642–652.

Stankov, L., Morony, S. and Lee, Y. P. (2014). Confidence: the best non-cognitive predictor of academic achievement? *Educational Psychology* 34: 9–28.

Strauss, L. and Volkwein, F. (2002). Comparing student performance and growth in 2- and 4-year institutions. *Research in Higher Education* 43(2): 133–161.

Syed, M. (2017). *The Greatest: The Quest for Sporting Perfection* (London: Hodder & Stoughton).

Tangney, J. P., Baumeister, R. F. and Boone, A. L. (2004). High self-control predicts good adjustment, less pathology, better grades, and interpersonal success. *Journal of Personality* 72(2): 271–324.

Tough, P. (2016). *Helping Children Succeed: What Works and Why* (London: Penguin Random House).

Treadaway, M. (2015). Why measuring pupil progress involves more than taking a straight line. *Education Datalab* (5 March). Available at: https://educationdatalab.org.uk/2015/03/ why-measuring-pupil-progress-involves-more-than-taking-a-straight-line/.

Trouilloud, D., Sarrazin, P., Martinek, T. and Guillet, E. (2002). The influence of teacher expectations on students' achievement in physical education classes: Pygmalion revisited. *European Journal of Social Psychology* 32(5): 591–607.

Whitmore, J. (2009). *Coaching for Performance, GROWing Human Potential and Purpose: The Principles and Practice of Coaching and Leadership*, 3rd edn (London: Nicholas Brealey).

Wiley, L. S. (1998). *Comprehensive Character-Building Classrooms: A Handbook for Teachers* (Manchester, NH: Character Development Foundation).

Wiseman, R. (2015). *59 Seconds: Think a Little, Change a Lot* (London: Pan Macmillan).

Wood, P. and Smith, J. (2016). *Educational Research: Taking the Plunge* (Carmarthen: Independent Thinking Press).

Yeager, D. S. and Walton, G. M. (2011). Social-psychological interventions in education: they're not magic. *Review of Educational Research* 81: 267–301.

Yeager, D. S., Walton, G. M. and Cohen, G. L. (2013). Addressing achievement gaps with psychological interventions. *Phi Delta Kappan* 94(5): 62–65.

Zimmerman, B. J. (2000). The impact of self-efficacy, achievement motivation, self-regulated learning strategies on pupils' academic achievement. *Procedia-Social and Behavioural Sciences* 15: 2623–2626.

Zimmerman, B. J. (2001). Theories of self-regulated learning and academic achievement: an overview and analysis. In B. J. Zimmerman and D. H. Schunk (eds), *Self-Regulated Learning and Academic Achievement: Theoretical Perspectives*, 2nd edn (Mahwah, NJ: Lawrence Erlbaum), pp. 1–38.

Zimmerman, B. J. and Ringle, J. (1981). Effects of model persistence and statements of confidence on children's efficacy and problem solving. *Journal of Educational Psychology* 73(4): 485–493.

Index

action plan 22, 147
action steps 60–61, 186–187
agency 97–99, 100–101, 202
Allcott, G. 74
Areepattamannil, S. 11
attention 12, 74–75, 133, 174
    active 74–75, 133
    inactive 74–75
    proactive 74–75
attitude (A) 15, 17, 18,26–29, 97,
    192, 216, 227–228
    of VESPA 27
attitude (A) activities
    Battery, The 107
    Benefit Finding, aka The
      Rocky Road 168
    First Aid Kit – Three
      Exercises to Dissolve
      Stress, The 175
    Growth Mindset 47
    Managing Reactions to
      Feedback 111
    Network Audits 76
    Problem Solving Cycle, The
      136
Azevedo, R. 21

Baizhan, L. 159
Bandura, A. 9, 99–100
Belsky, S. 199
Berkowitz, M. W. 1
Bier, M. C. 1

Binet, A. 12
Birdwell, J. 194
Blue Coat School, The 216
Bolt, U. 127
Brackett, M. 9–10
Bull, S. 107, 111
buoyancy 10–11, 27 *see also*
    resilience

Campbell, M. A. 182
Canfield, J. 60
Carey, B. 140, 161
Cepeda, N. J. 140
change 31–33, 37, 47–48, 52,
    59, 78–79, 85, 111, 117–118,
    154, 172, 181, 184–185, 187,
    196–198
Change Curve 31–33, 53
Changing Lanes 152–154,
    156–158
character (C) 1–13, 193–195,
    225
    building blocks of character
      5
Cirillo, F. 125
Clements-Croome, D. 159
coach record sheet 186
coaching 181–192
    conversations 98, 100, 182,
      184–187
    questions 187–192
Cohen, G. 196

Collins, D. 168–169
Collins, J. 78
comfort zone 18, 26, 93
conscientiousness 7, 9–10
content 12, 29, 84–85, 149, 152,
    195, 227
    validity 215
conversation 34, 95–96, 117,
    131–135, 181 *see also*
    coaching; conversations
      goal setting 36
Cooper, H. 68–69, 117
Covey, S. R. 145, 177
Csikszentmihalyi, M. 150–152

Dagnall, N. 34, 212
deadlines 24, 52, 183, 190
Denovan, A. 34, 212
Dewar, M. 25
Dilts, R. B. 133, 134
Dilts' Disney Method 133, 134
distractions 26, 41, 44, 57, 115,
    116, 123
dream 60
Duckworth, A. 8–9, 19, 20,
    22–23, 64–65, 66
Dweck, C. 8, 19, 47, 187, 205
    Dweck's mindset
      questionnaire 8, 47–48

efficacy 97–98, 99–101 *see also*
    self-efficacy

Index

effort (E) 2, 8, 12, 15, 17–18, 22–24, 25, 100, 113–129, 209, 216, 226
    1–10 scale, the 23
effort (E) activities
    Effort Thermometer, The 119
    Looking Under the Rocks, aka Four Steps Forward 78
    Mission and Medal 43
    Packing My Bags 121
    Pre-Making Decisions 178
    Three 'Hows' of Independent Work, The 88
    Twenty-Five Minute Sprints 123
Emmons, R. A. 168
Ericsson, A. 22, 26

failure 8, 9, 22, 100, 154, 168, 200
    fear of 1, 8, 32, 100, 154
Farrington, C. A. 11–12
fear 29, 53, 97, 153 see also failure; fear of
feedback 8, 18, 26–29, 68–69, 83, 85, 87, 99–100, 111–112, 116, 143, 150, 153, 187, 199, 202, 215
    loop 28–29, 69, 210
Ferriss, T. 176, 177
fixed mindset 8, 47, 97, 154, 209
Flavell, J. H. 11
flow 69, 149–161, 227
    flow model 151
Flutter, J. 202

Gantt charts 207
Gardner, S. 182

GCSE Mindset Questionnaire 216–223
Geirland, J. 150
Gladwell, M. 22
Glaser, B. 16
goal setting 18, 19–21, 29, 36–38, 56–57, 93–94, 144–146, 215, 226
Godin, S. 54, 227–228
Goldberg, L. R. 9
Good, T. 69, 117
Graham, P. 53, 54
Griffin, M. 216,
grit 7, 8–9, 11, 20, 64–66, 194, 196, 202
Grit Scale 9–10, 64–66
Gross-Loh, C. 8
growth mindset 7, 8, 15, 26, 27, 29, 47–49, 194
Gutman, L. M. 6, 10, 16

habit(s) 4, 12, 13, 25, 57, 69, 122, 172–174, 185, 216
    habit breaking 122
    habit formation 13, 46, 97, 114–118, 122, 172–174, 183
    habit of effort 43–46, 225, 226
Harrison, T. 203, 208
Hassanbeigi, A. 25
Heckman, J. J. 1, 6, 9, 22
Higher Education Statistics Agency 196
Holiday, R. 144

IAG (information, advice and guidance) 36–37
implementation 193–211, 216

independent study 15, 24, 82–85, 114–116, 216, 228 see also revision
indicators 67–81
    lagging indicators 68–69, 135
    leading indicators 69–70, 115, 135, 226
influences 51–52
    external 52–53
    internal 53
    unexpected 52, 53
intervention conversation 184–192
Ivcevic, Z. 9–10

Jacobson, L. 117
Jerusalem, M. 100
Jubilee Centre for Character and Virtues 4–5, 193, 193–194, 202–203, 207–208
Jung, Y. 24
justification, pupil's 133–134

Kautz, T. 6, 9, 22
Key Stage 1 3
Key Stage 2 3
Key Stage 3 3, 62
Key Stage 4 2, 3, 13, 15, 16, 33, 35, 68, 101, 195
Key Stage 5 2, 3, 15, 16, 149
Khine, M. S. 11
Kolb, D. 132, 136
Kotler, S. 150
KPMG 36
Kübler-Ross, E. 31–32, 53

Landsberg, M. 127
laziness 57, 117

Lee, J. 26
Lincoln, A. 162

McCabe, P. 100
McCullough, M. E. 168
McGahan, J. 142–143
McGeown, S. 1
MacGilchrist, B. 202
McKeen Catell, J. 213
McLeod, S. 132
MacNamara, A. 168
mantra 172
Mapping Trouble 53–56
Margolis, H. 100
Marsh, H. 10
Martin, A. J. 10, 93
mastery 47, 136, 187
meta-cognition 11–12, 17
mindset 8, 19, 47–49, 196–197,
    199, 200, 204, 208–210
    fixed *see* fixed mindset
    growth *see* growth mindset
    measuring mindset 211–223
    mindset intervention 202,
        204, 208
Mischel, W. 10
mistakes 26, 95
Mitra, D. L. 202
modelling 116, 135, 174
monitoring progress 11, 187
Moriarity, J. 21
motivation 5, 9, 21, 39–41
Muijs, D. 27
Multon, K. D. 9
'myth of effortless success' 24

National Foundation for
    Educational Research 182
Newport, C. 90

non-cognitive constructs 7–11
non-cognitive skills 1–13, 15–19,
    31, 193–210, 225–228
normalising effort 23, 114, 174

Oakes, S. 216
Oettingen, G. 105
organisation skills 3, 9–10,
    25–26, 90–91, 115, 125–126

perfomance 2–6, 23–24, 68–70,
    117, 132–133, 150, 182, 184,
    214–216
planning 185, 206–208
Pool, R. 22
Poropat, A. E. 9
practical wisdom 5
practice (P) 15, 17, 18, 25–26,
    81–97, 191, 216, 227
    deliberate practice 15, 26,
        29
    practice questionnaire 86–87
    Three Phases of Practice,
        the 81–97
practice (P) activities
    Building Independent
        Learning 71
    Finding Flow 155
    High Flow Spaces 159
    It's Time to Teach, aka
        CASTT 90
    K-SPA 138
    Nine-Box Grid, The 125
    Practice Questionnaire, The
        86
    Spaced Practice 140
    Test Yourself! 142
    Will vs. Skill 127
Price, A. 104, 138

Price, D. 104
prioritising 162–167, 226–227
'problem and purpose' 37–38
procrastination 88
psychometric tests 211–223
'pull goal' 21
'push goal' 21

recall 90–92, 140–143
    active recall 90–92
    passive recall 90
reflecting 20
Reiss, S. 39–40
resilience 4, 5, 7, 10–11, 37, 69
    see also buoyancy
revision 18, 26, 58–59, 82,
    86–89, 90, 95–96, 125–129,
    140–143, 154, 191 *see also*
    independent study
    revision questionnaire 86–87
reward 10, 43, 56, 80, 115–116,
    117–118, 207
Reynolds, D. 27
Ringle, J. 99
Roediger, H. 142
Rohn, J. 95
Rosenthal, R. 117
Rowling, J. K. 64
Rubinstein, Y. 1
Rudduck, J. 202

Schoon, I. 6, 10, 16
Schunk, D. H. 9, 19
Schwarzer, R. 100
Seelig, T. 98–99
Seinfeld, J. 46
self-control 7, 10, 11, 18
self-efficacy 7, 9
self-knowledge 213, 226

Index

self-sabotage 53, 226

Sherman, D. 196

Simon, T. 12

Sivers, D. 37, 41

skill 22, 85, 127–129, 150, 225–227

    non-cognitive 6–12, 15–16, 193–195, 225

    study skills 24–25

SMART goal setting 21

Smith, J. 197

Smith, W. 119

Stafford, T. 25

Stankov, L. 26

Strauss, A. 16

Strauss, L. 24

student action steps 186

students

    breakthrough 2, 3–4, 225

    ceiling 2, 3–4, 225

stress 151, 168, 171–179

Syed, M. 196

systems (S) 15, 17, 18, 25, 69–70, 190, 225, 226–227

systems (S) activities

    Action Priority Matrix, The 165

    Bottom Left, The 109

Chunking Steps 62

Three Types of Attention 74

Weekly Planner, The 58

Tangney, J. P. 10

Think Productive 74

time management 25–26, 58–59, 88–89, 165–167

Tough, P. 12

traits 5, 9–10

Treadaway, M. 3

Trouilloud, D. 117

US Department of Education 7

VESPA 15–30, 216–218

    audit 203–204

    implementation 193–210

    questionnaire 28, 34, 197, 198–199, 202, 205, 212, 218–220

    intervention 194–202, 205, 206

    model 17–18

    umbrella 16–17

    coaching with VESPA 181–192

virtues 4–6

vision (V) 15, 16, 17, 18, 19–22, 37, 184, 188, 198, 216, 226

vision (V) activities

    Five Roads 102

    Grit 64

    Motivation Diamond, The 39

    Now vs. Most 162

    Problem Not Job, aka The Personal Compass 41

    Roadmap, The 56

    Rule of Three, The 60

    Setting a Personal Best 93

    Success Leaves Clues 95

    Ten-Year Grid, The 104

    What's Stopping You? 144

visual reminder 56

Volkwein, F. 24

Walton, G. M. 195, 196, 197

well-being 171–179

Whitmore, J. 133, 181–182, 185

Wood, P. 197

Yeager, D. S. 8, 23, 195, 196, 197

Zimmerman, B. J. 29, 99